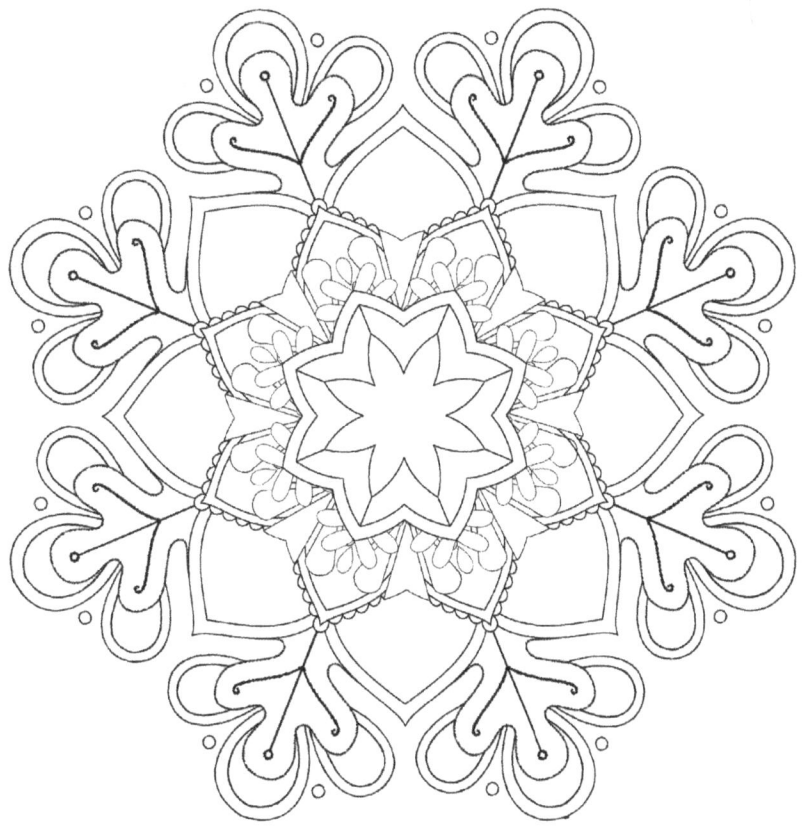

This
Coloring Book
Belongs to

Mandalas Art Therapy

Coloring mandalas leads to a relaxation response due to repetitive movement that forces us to put aside the thoughts that arise and return to the point of focus. The relaxation response of mandala coloring can result in the following benefits:
- Lower heart rate and blood pressure
- Reduced pulse rate
- Decreased oxygen consumption
- Increased release of feeling good hormones

Coloring a mandala with colored pencils, crayons, paint, or pastels combines the benefits of meditation and art therapy into a simple practice that can be done anytime anywhere.

People who color mandalas often experience a deep sense of tranquility and well-being.

It is a simple tool that does not require any experience, but it can be very comforting and nourishing. Mandalas not only focus your attention but also allow you to express your creative side, which many of us neglect in our daily lives.

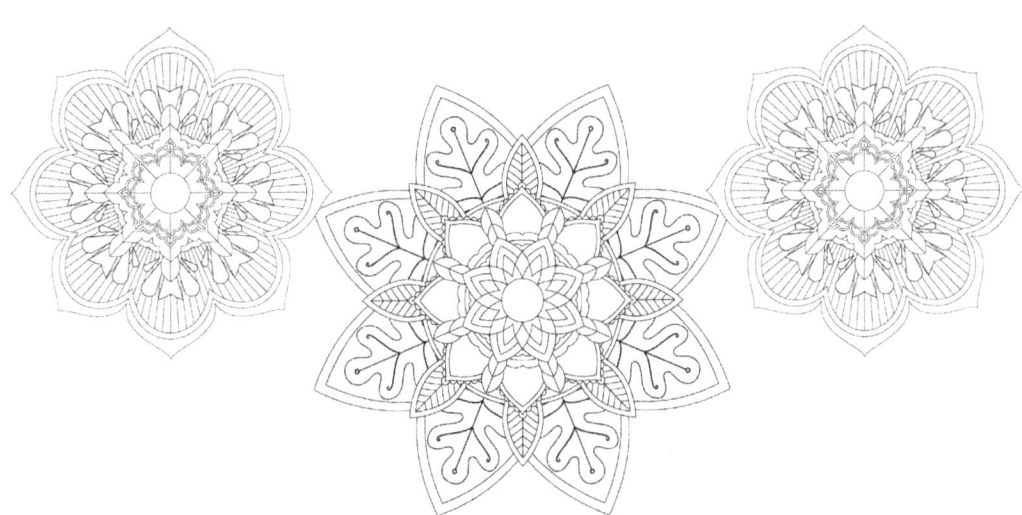

COLORS TEST

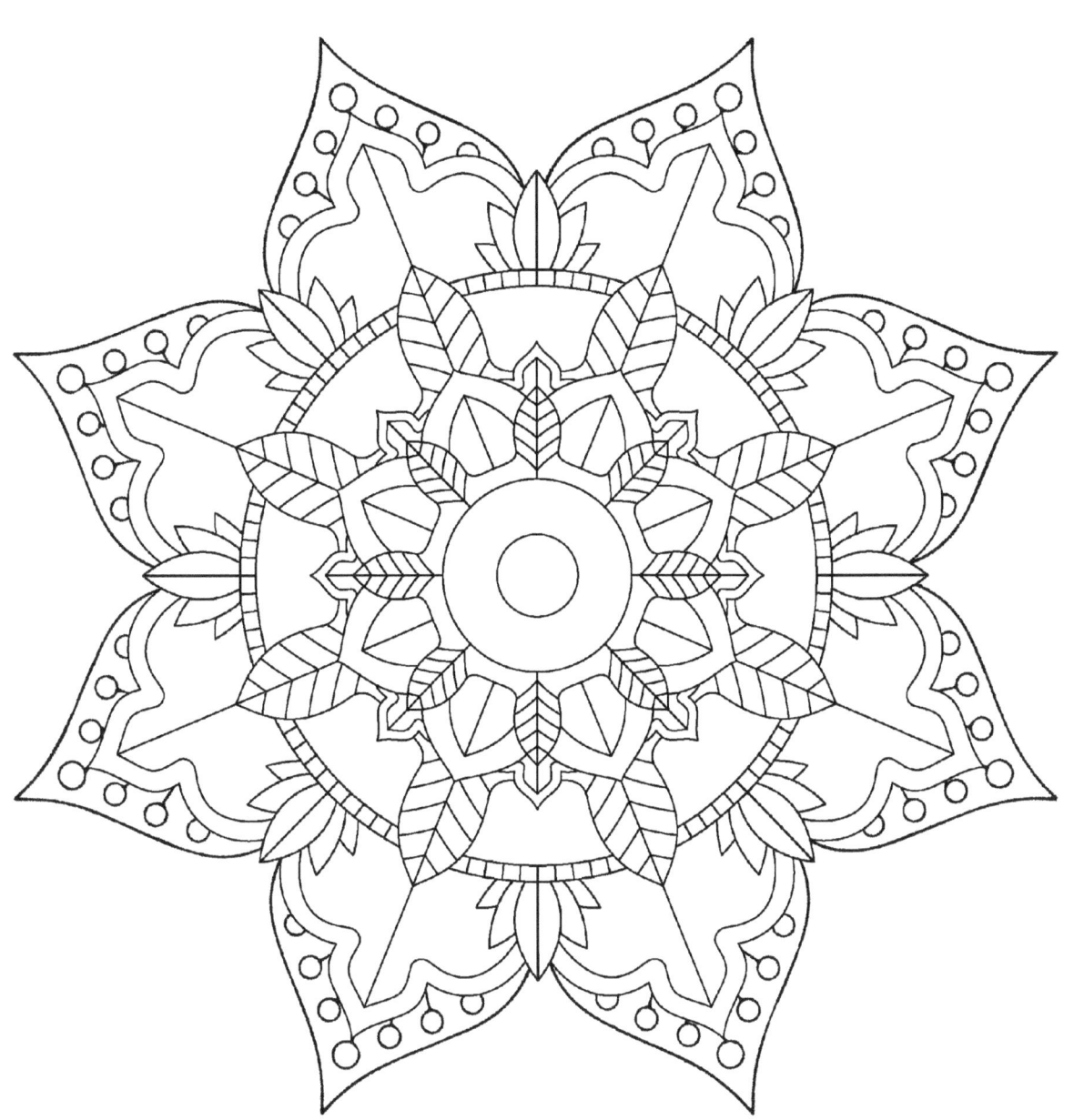

COLORS
TEST

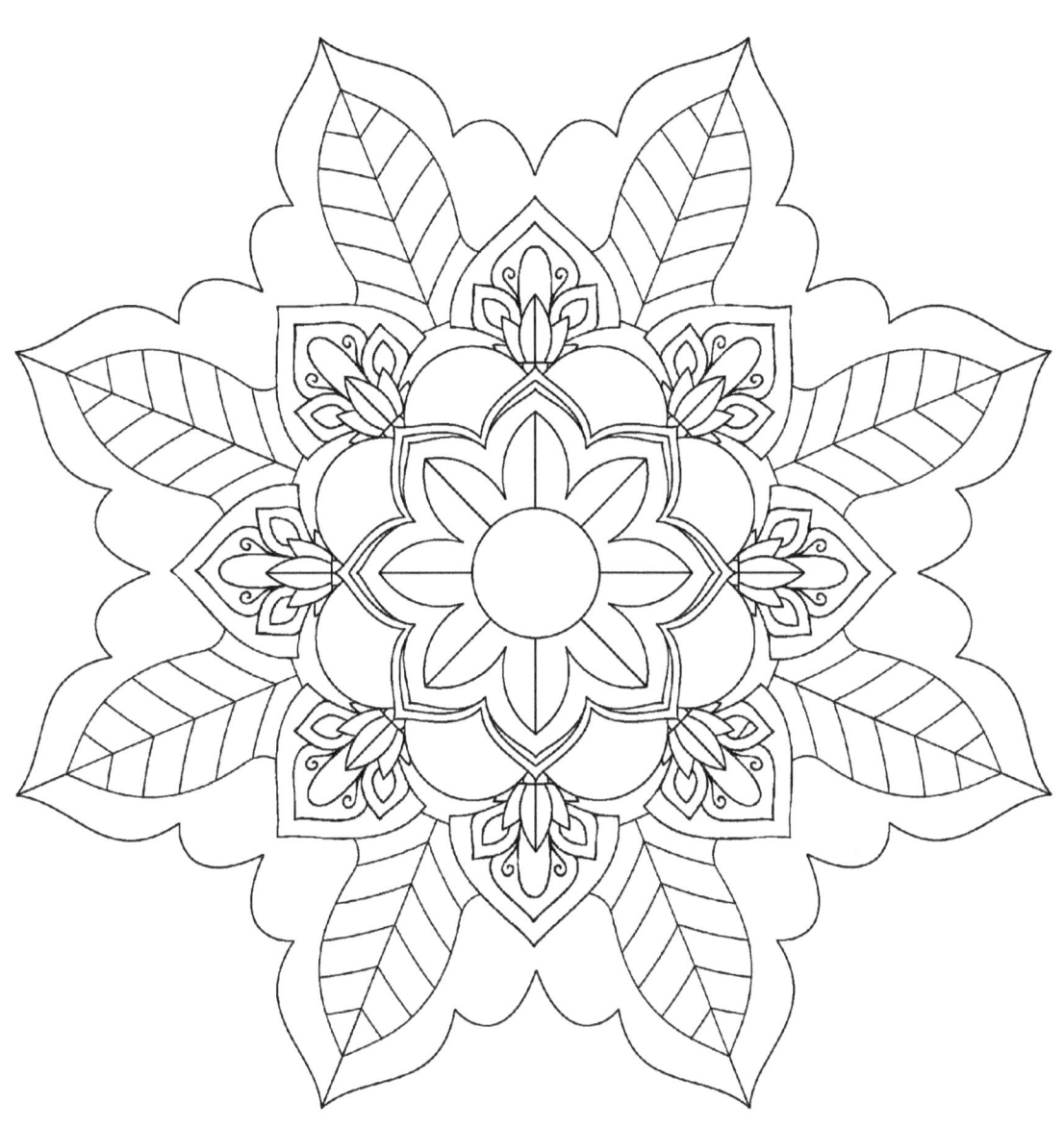

COLORS
TEST

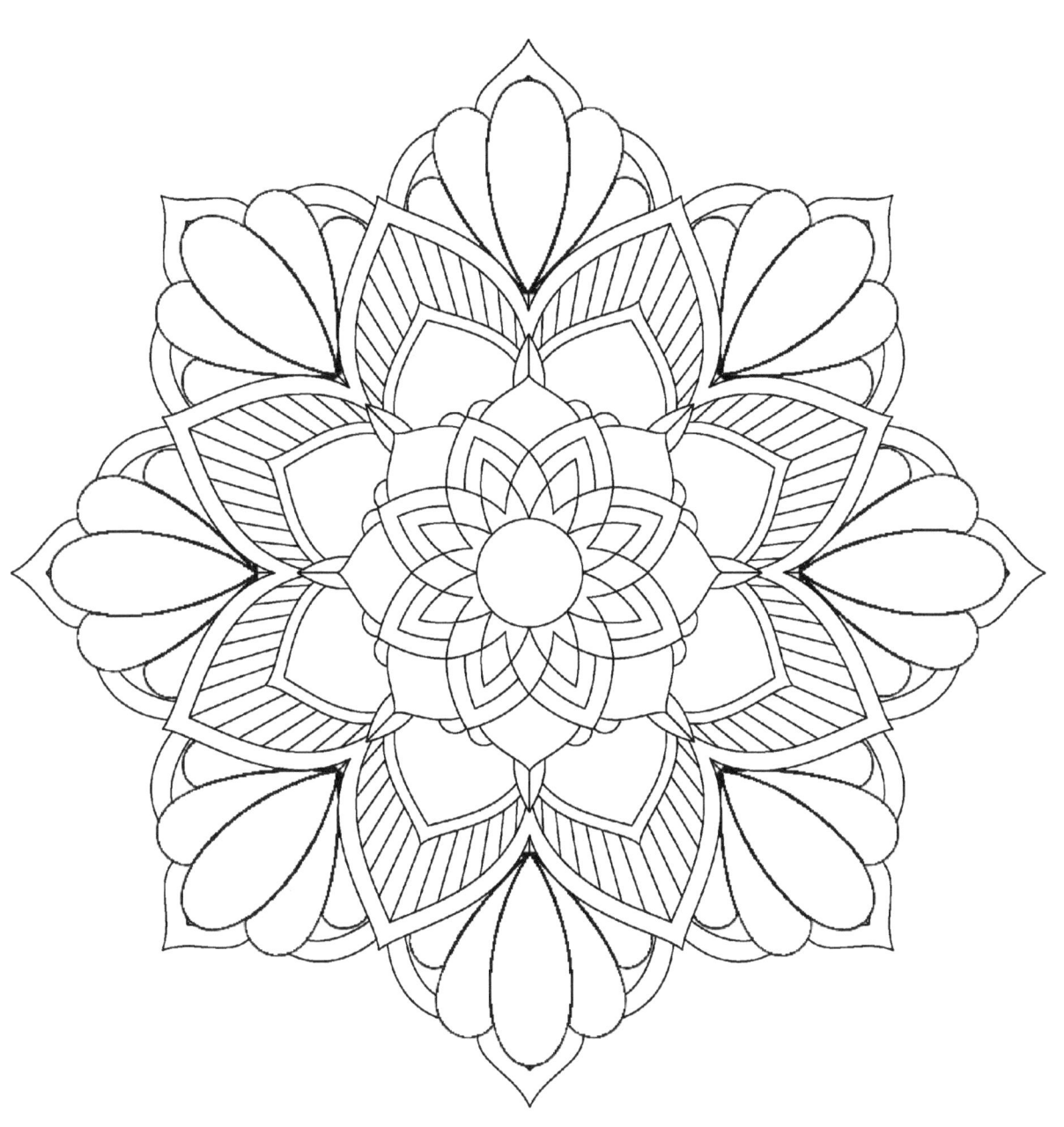

COLORS
TEST

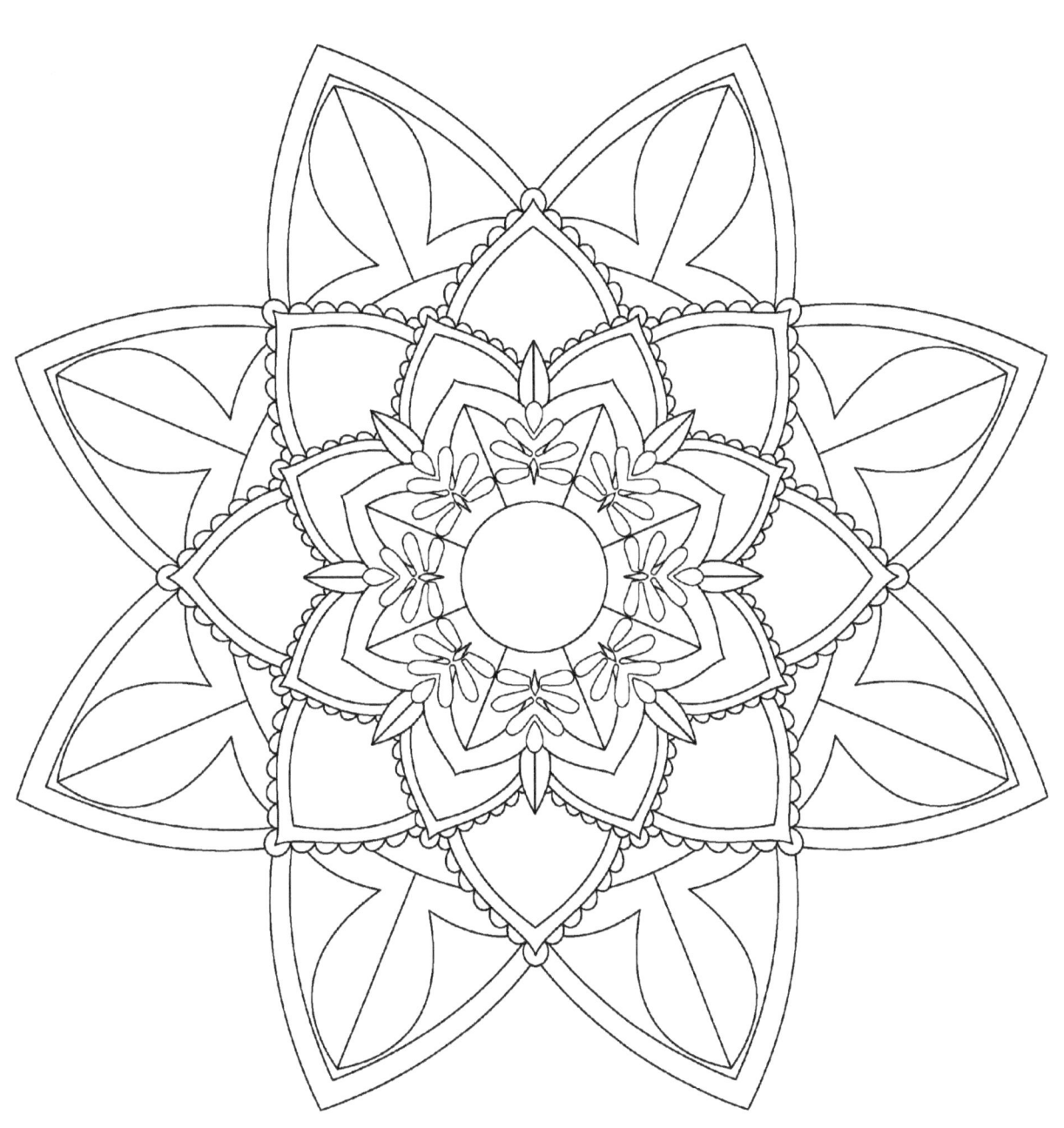

COLORS TEST

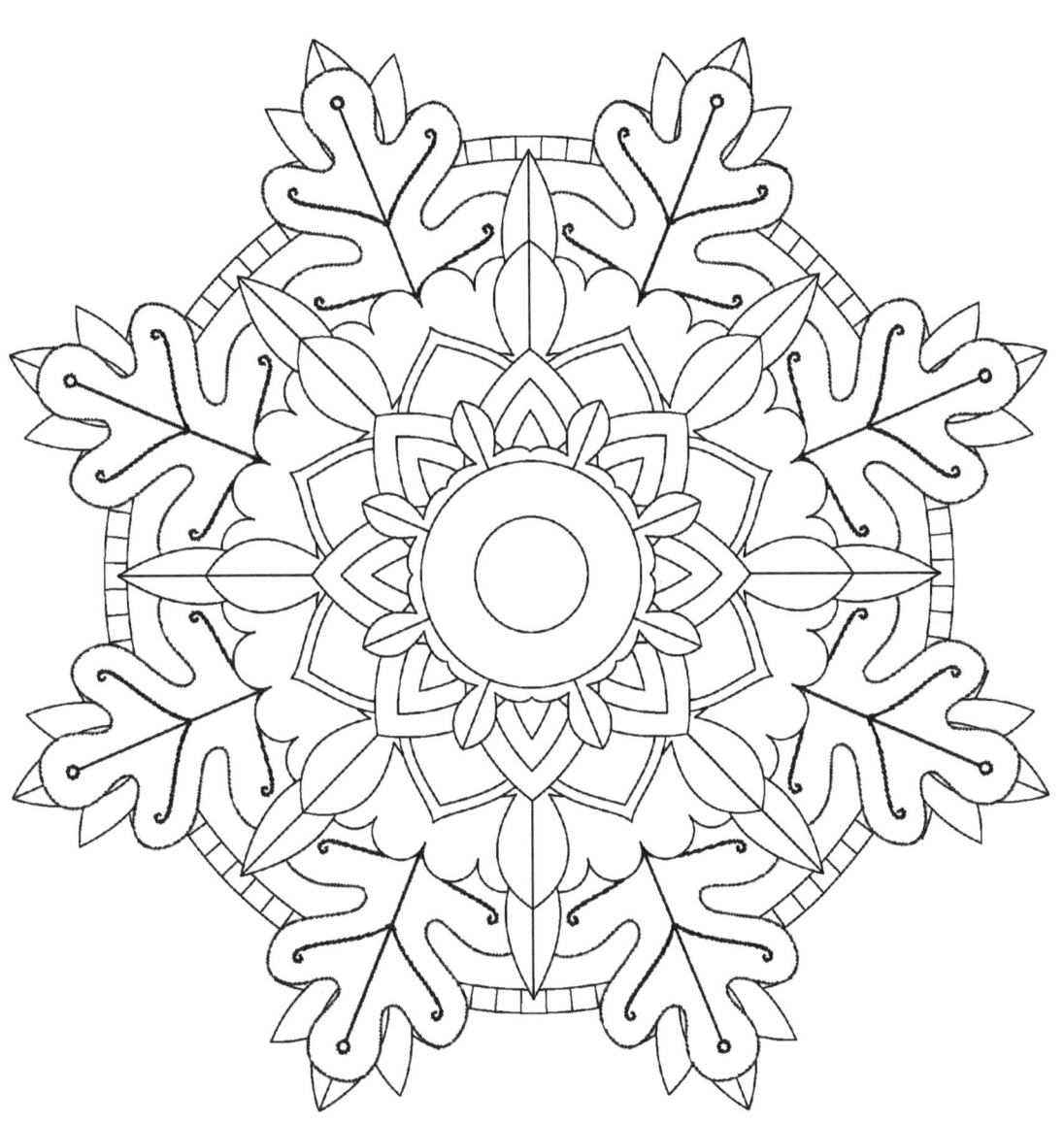

COLORS TEST

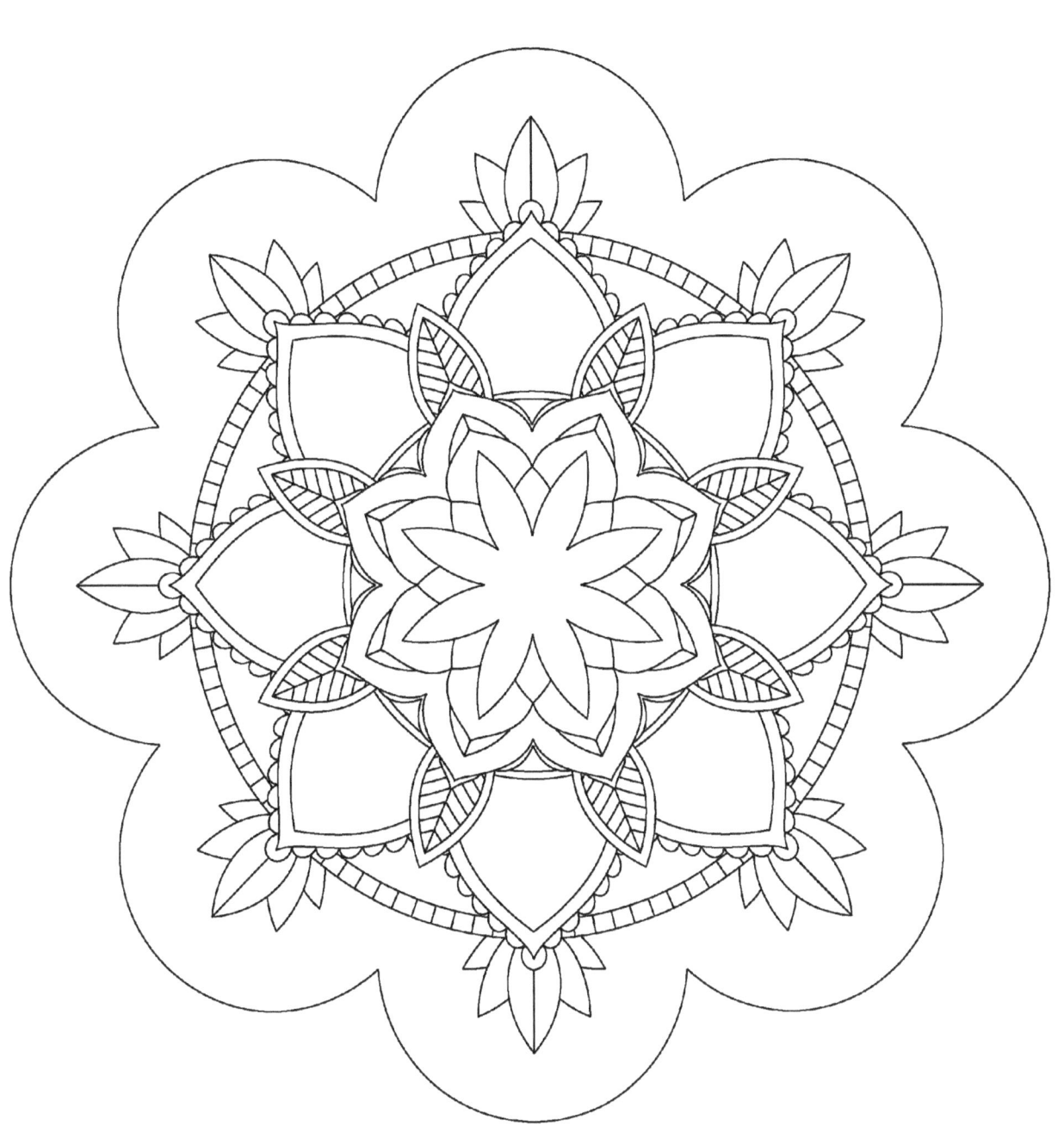

COLORS
TEST

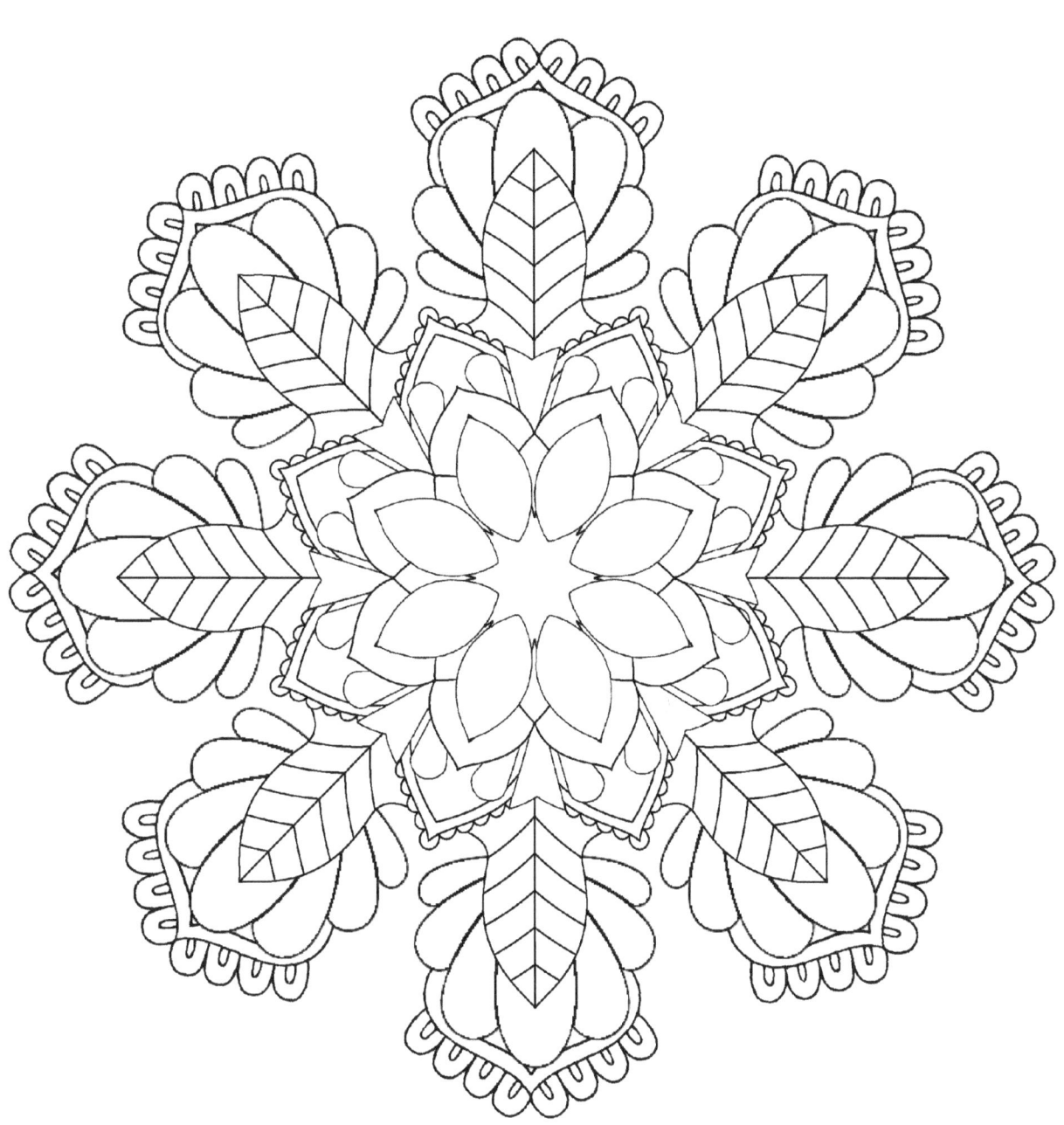

COLORS
TEST

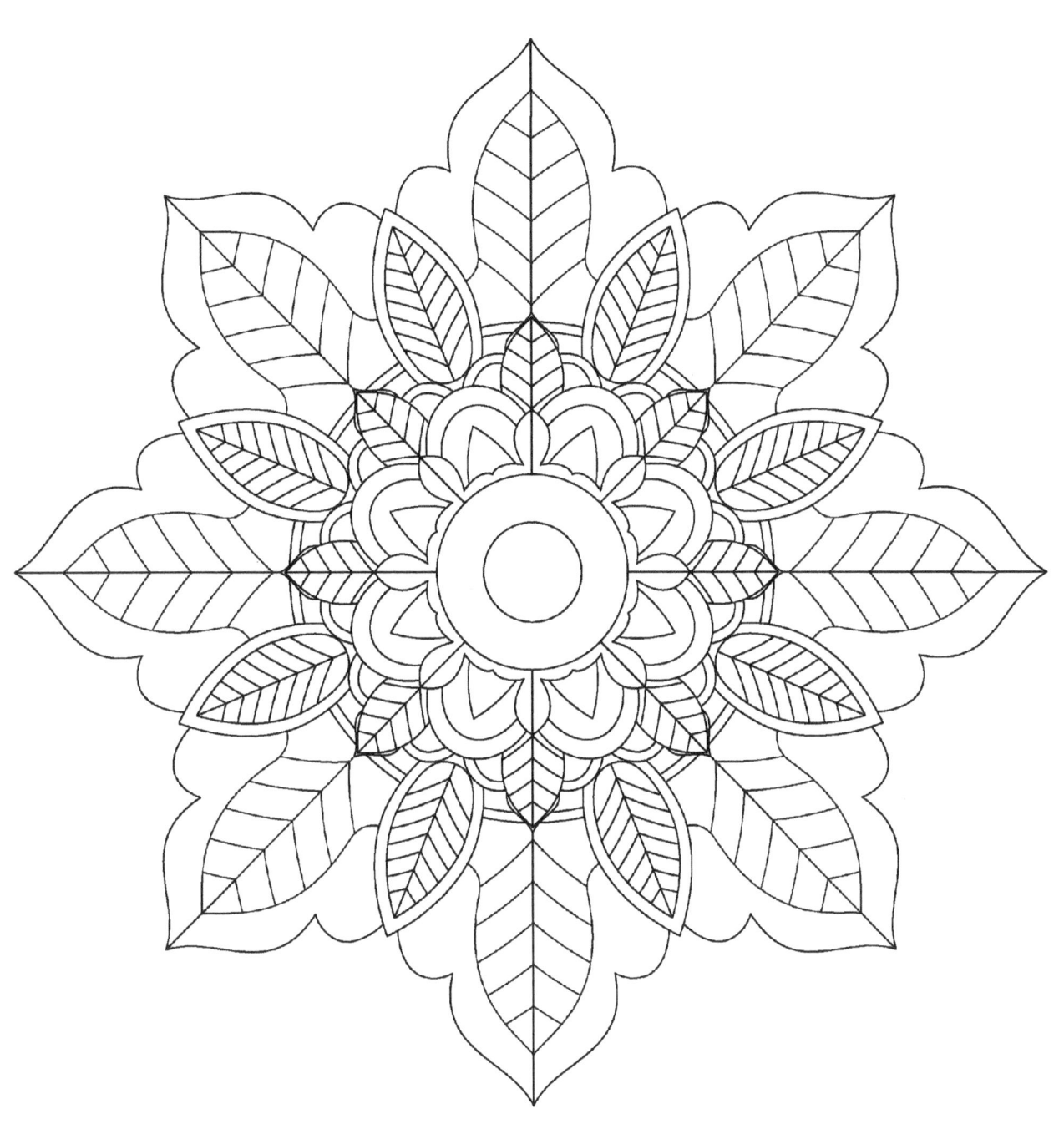

COLORS
TEST

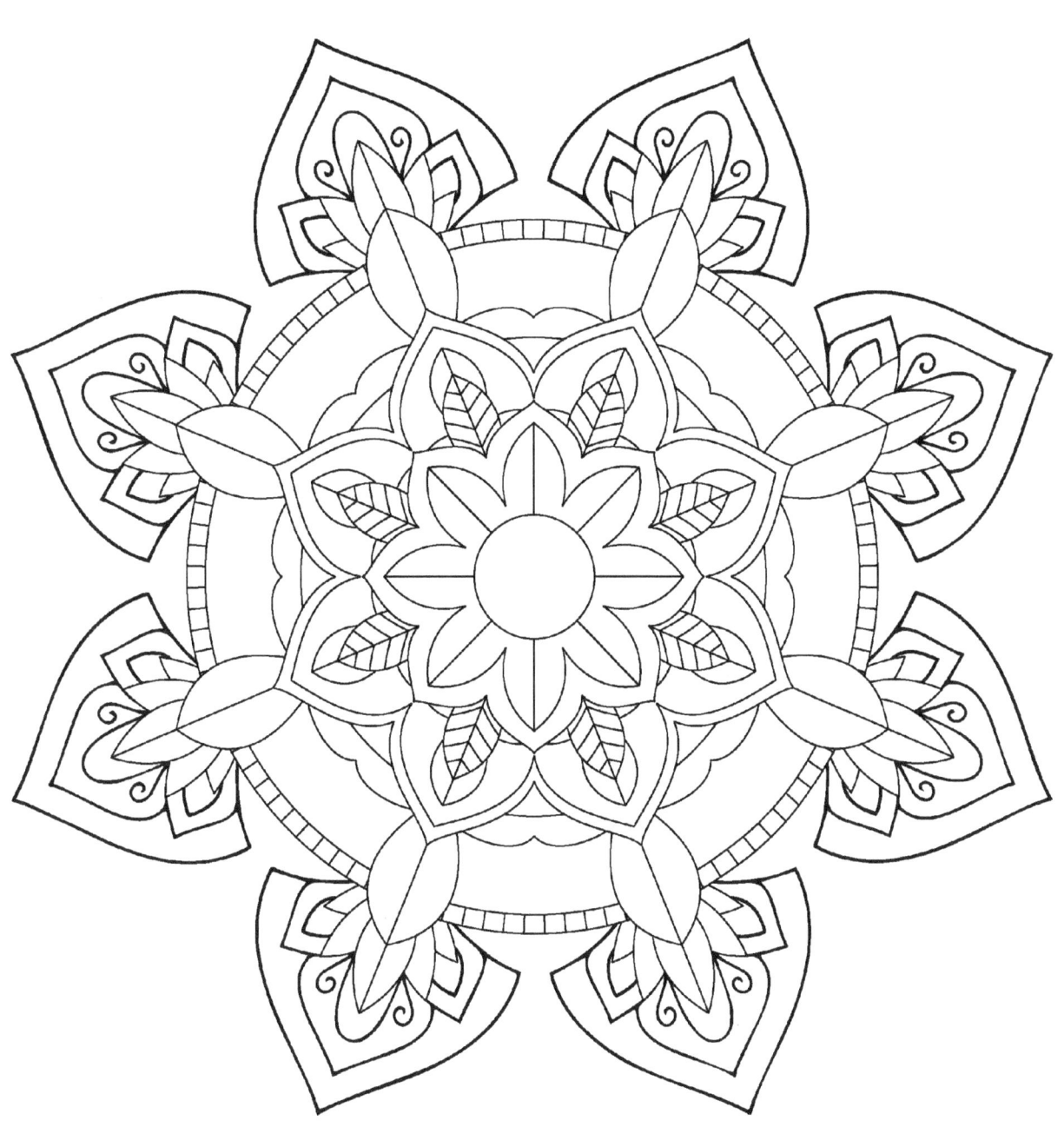

COLORS
TEST

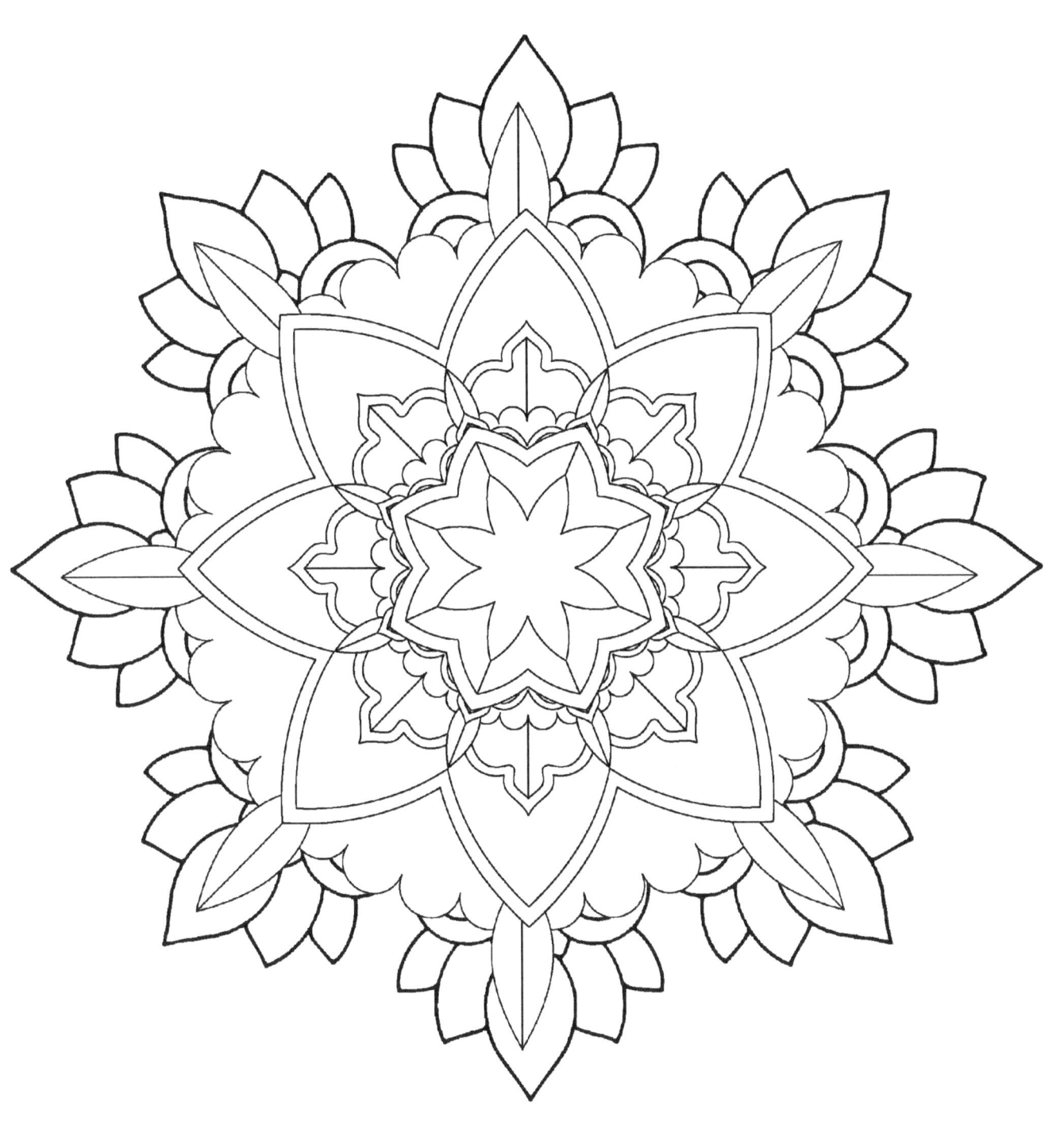

COLORS TEST

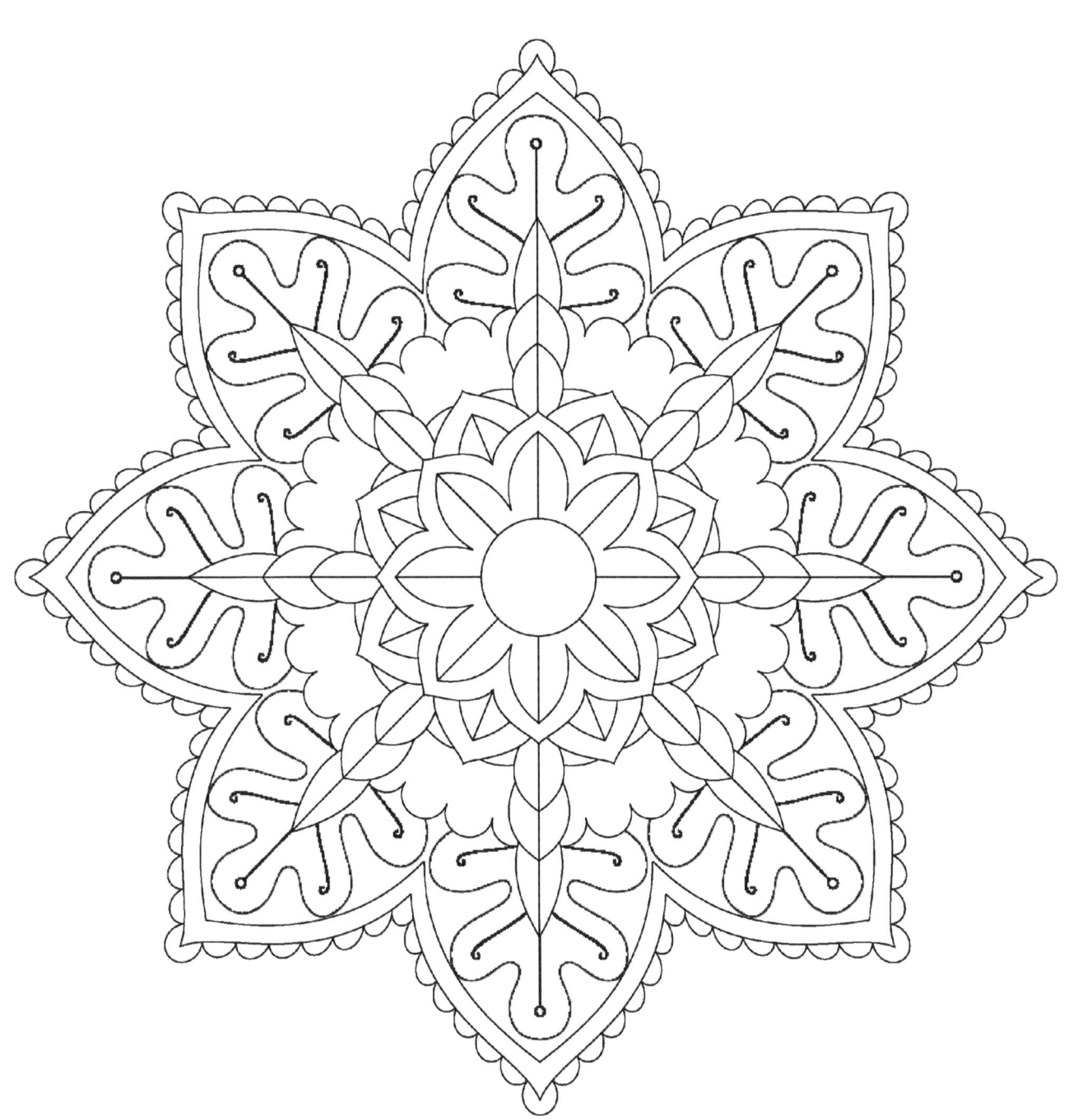

COLORS
TEST

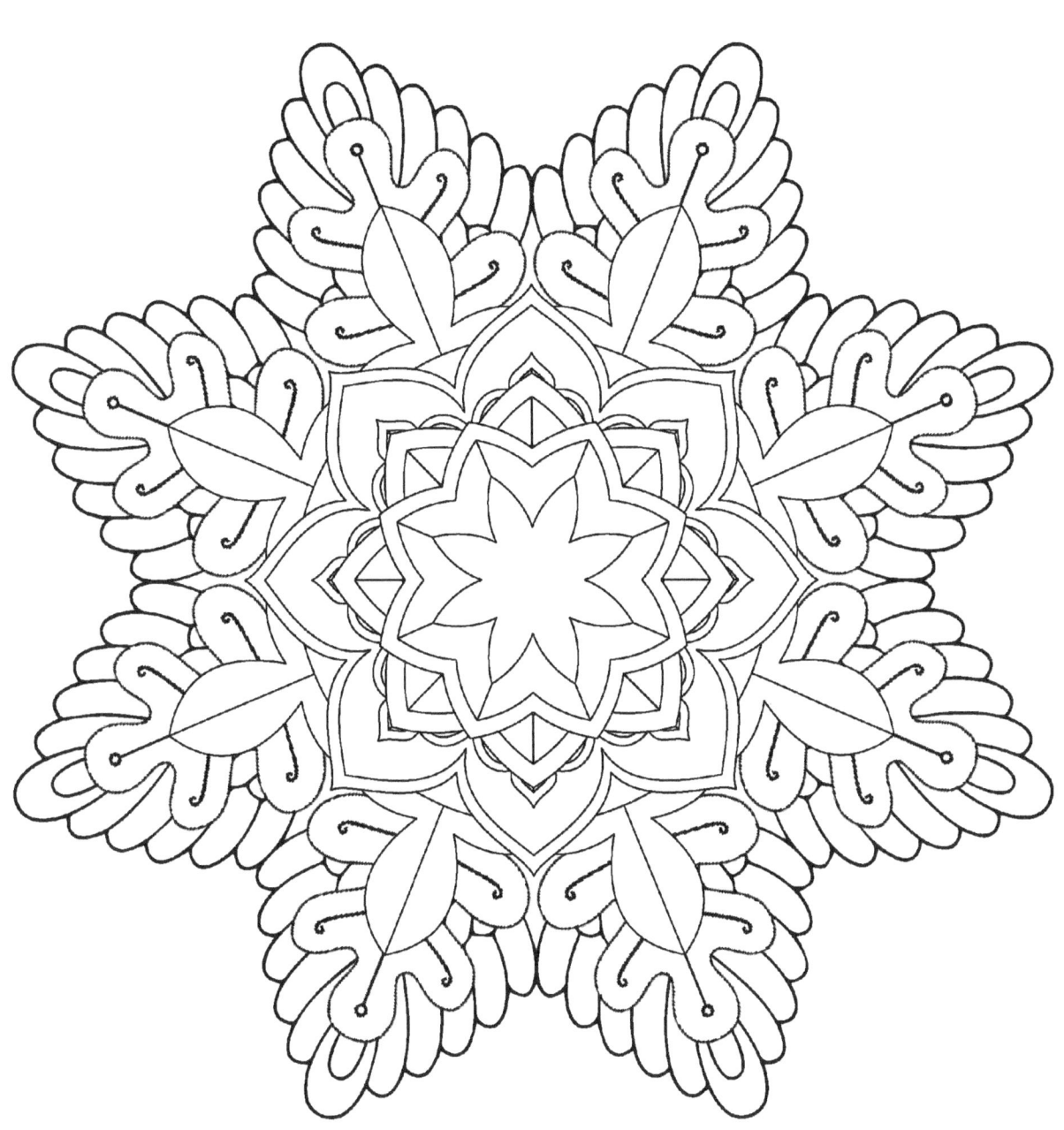

COLORS
TEST

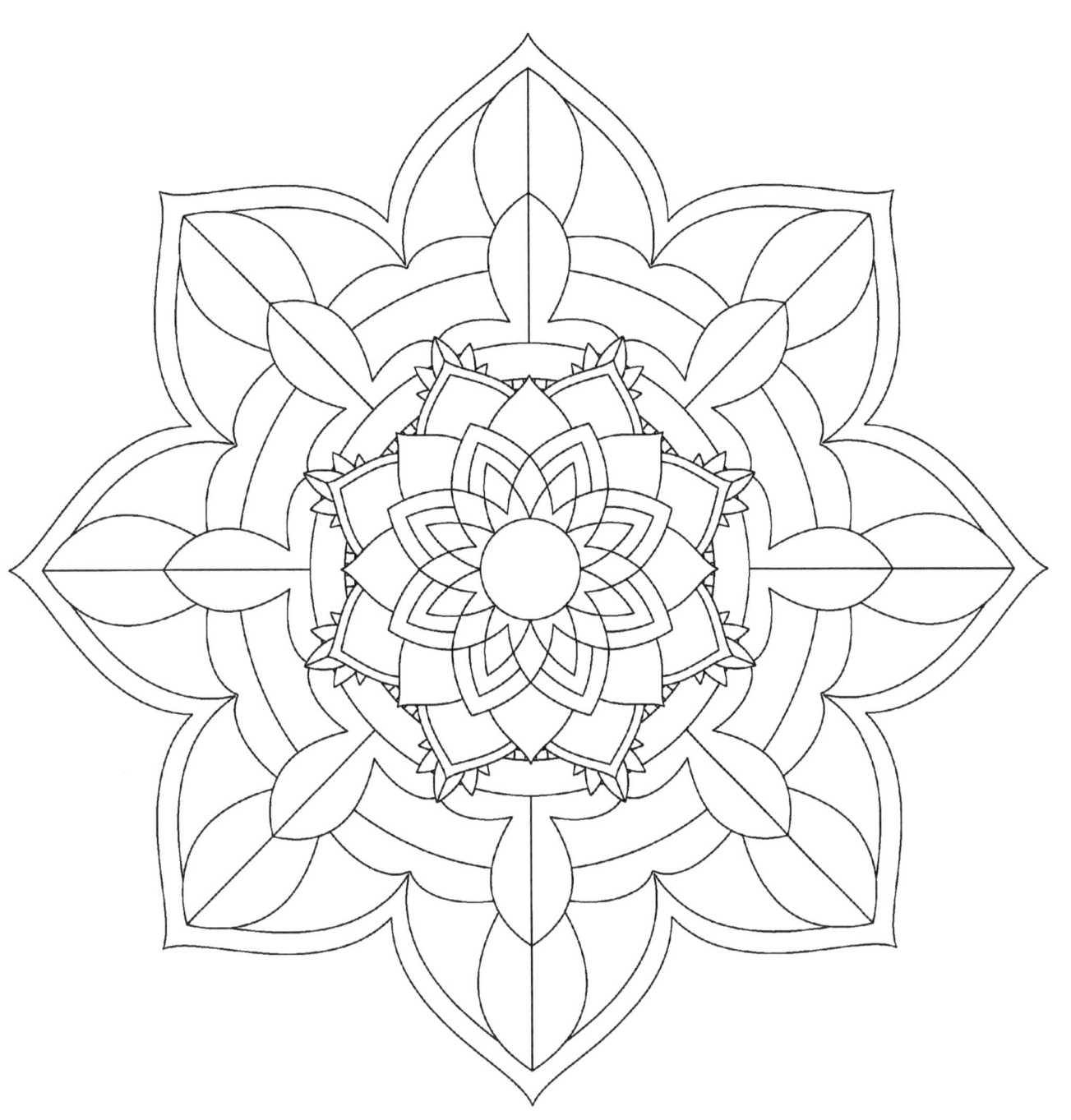

COLORS TEST

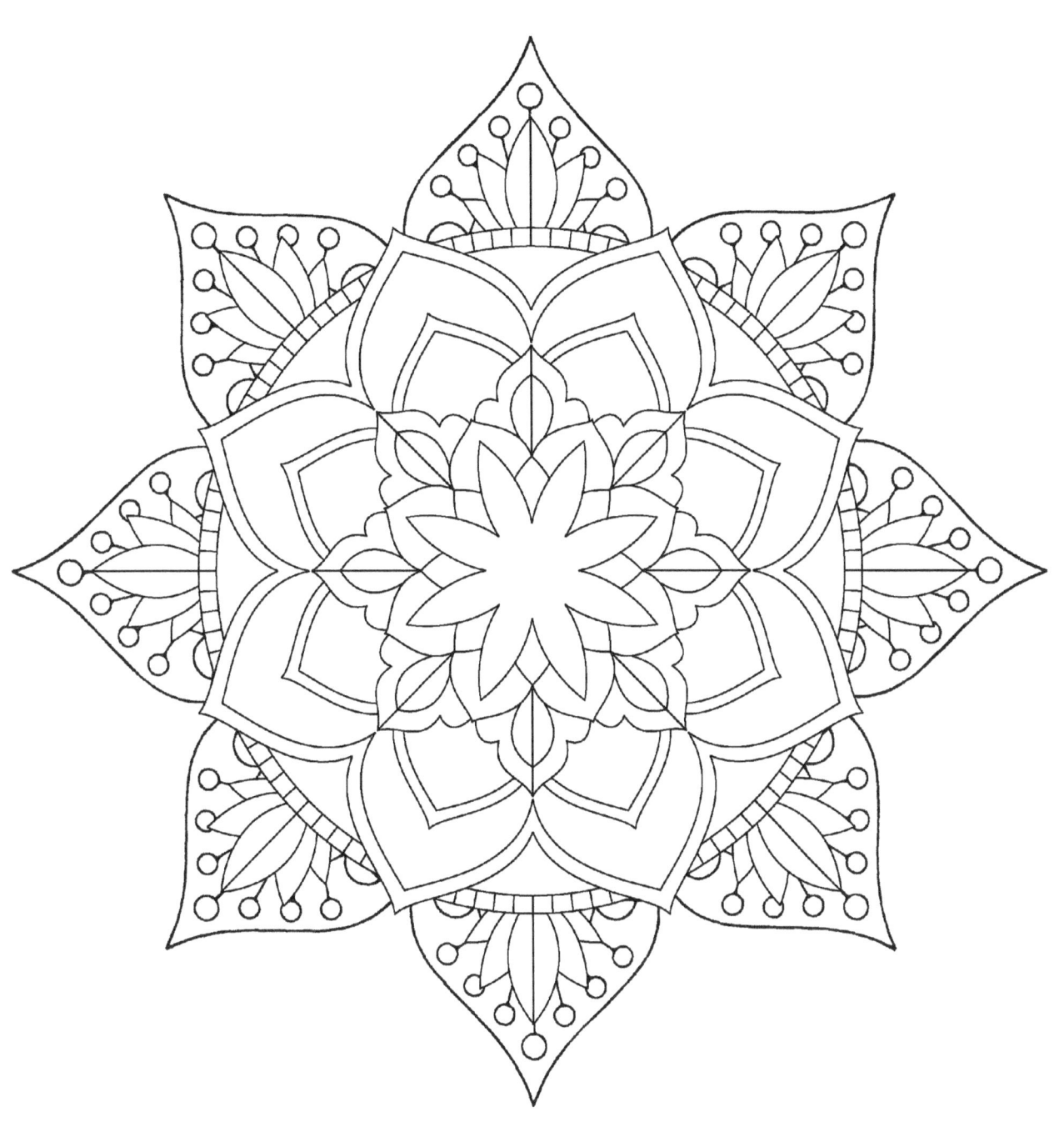

COLORS TEST

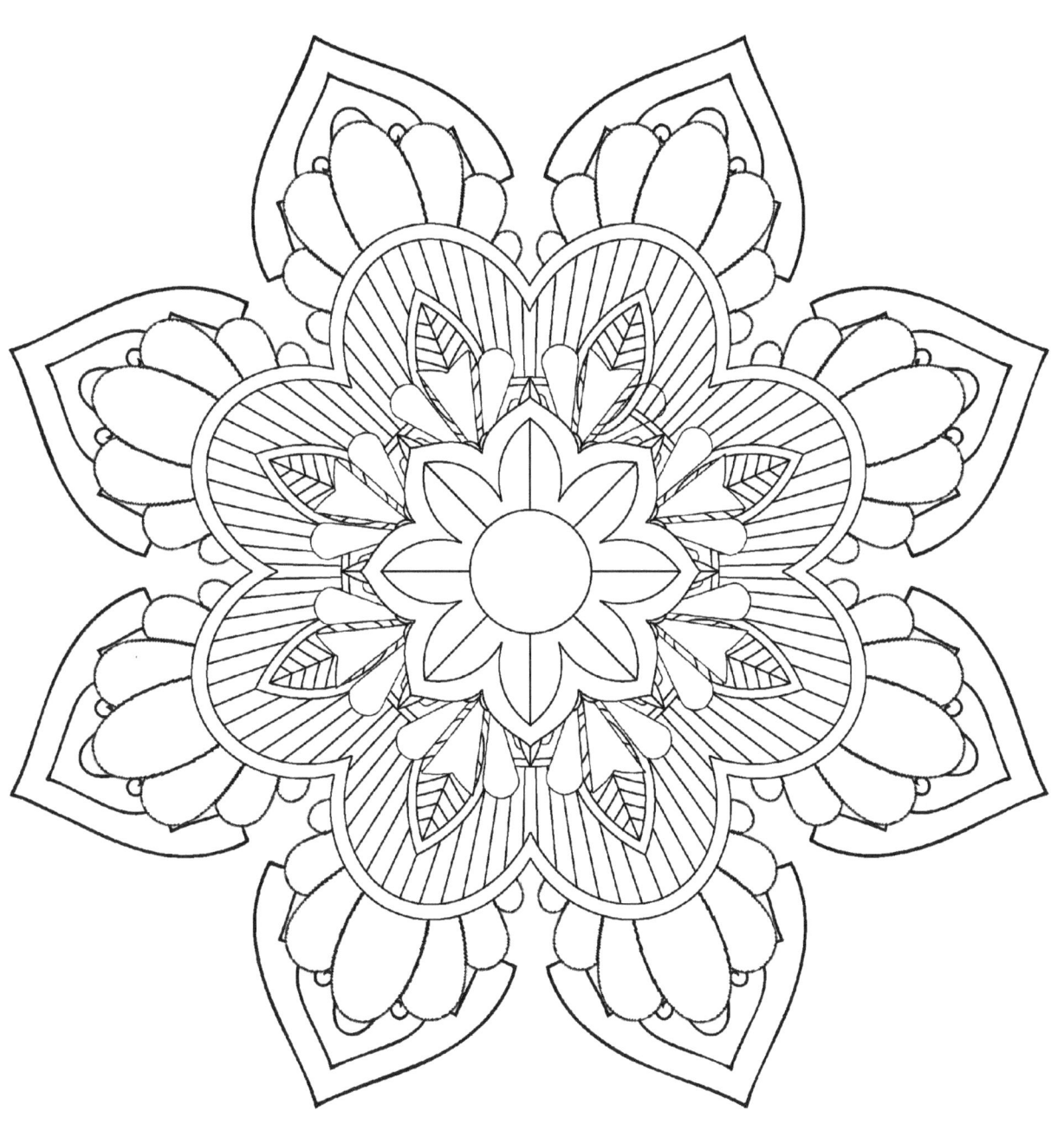

COLORS
TEST

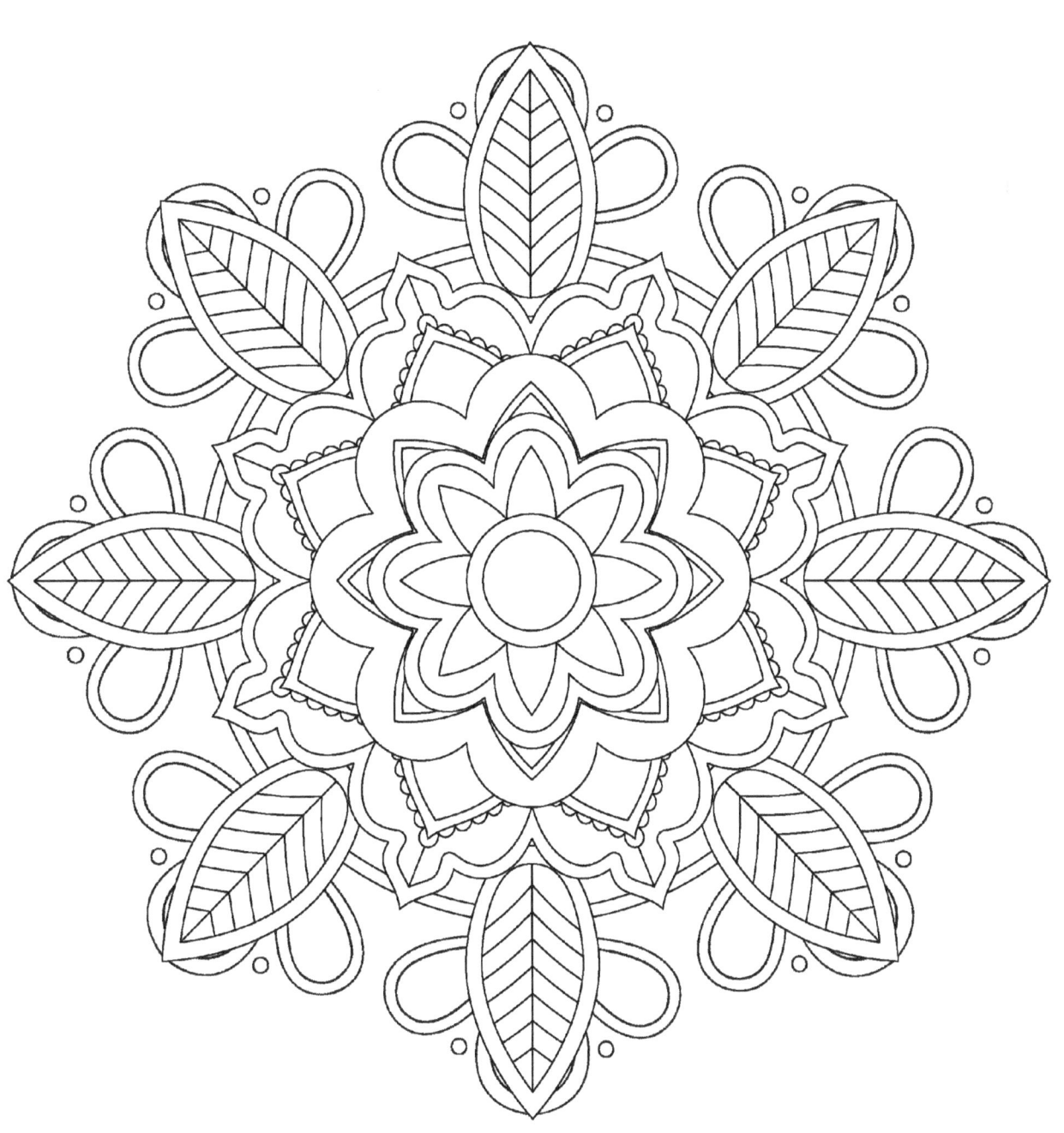

COLORS
TEST

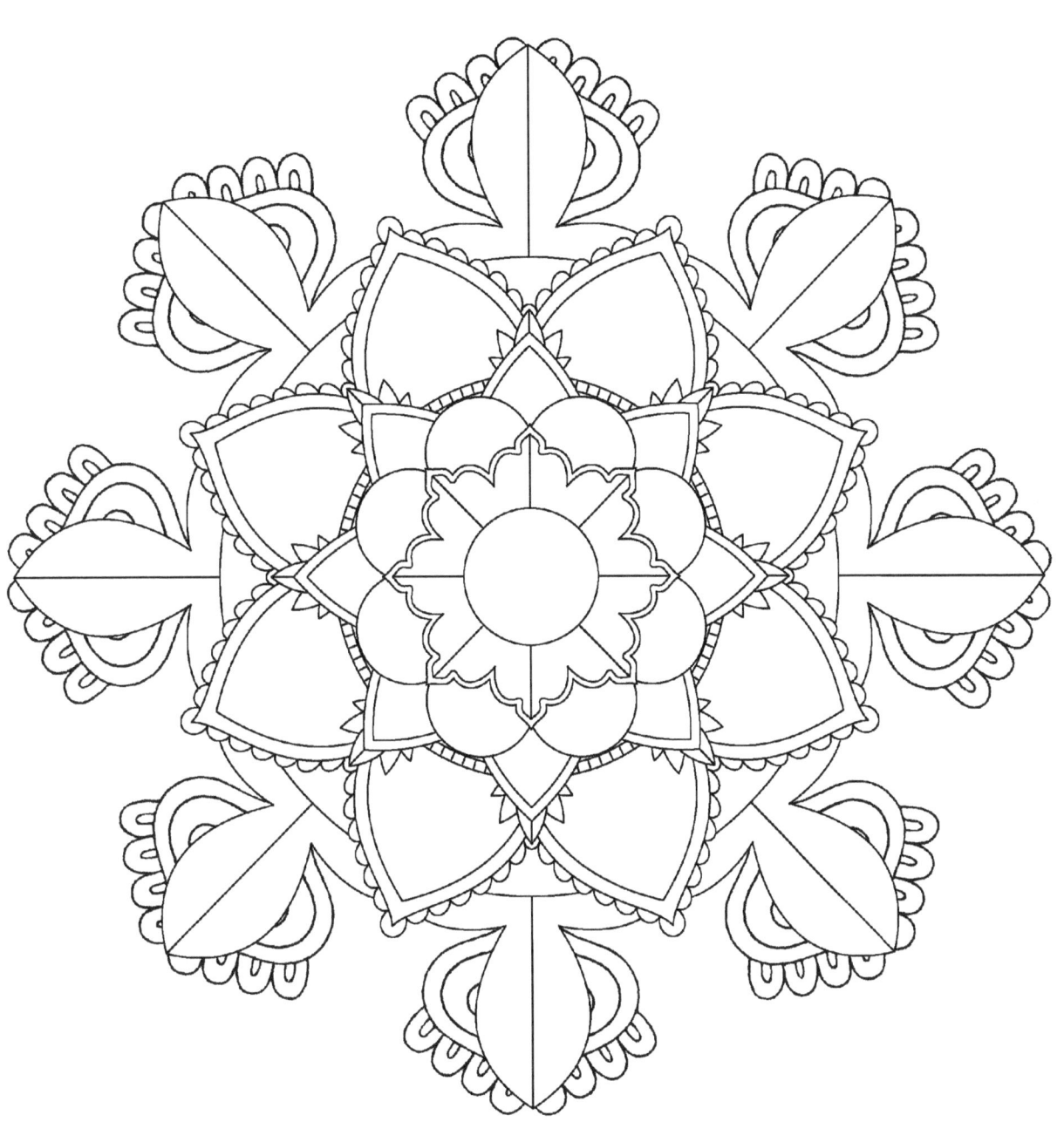

COLORS
TEST

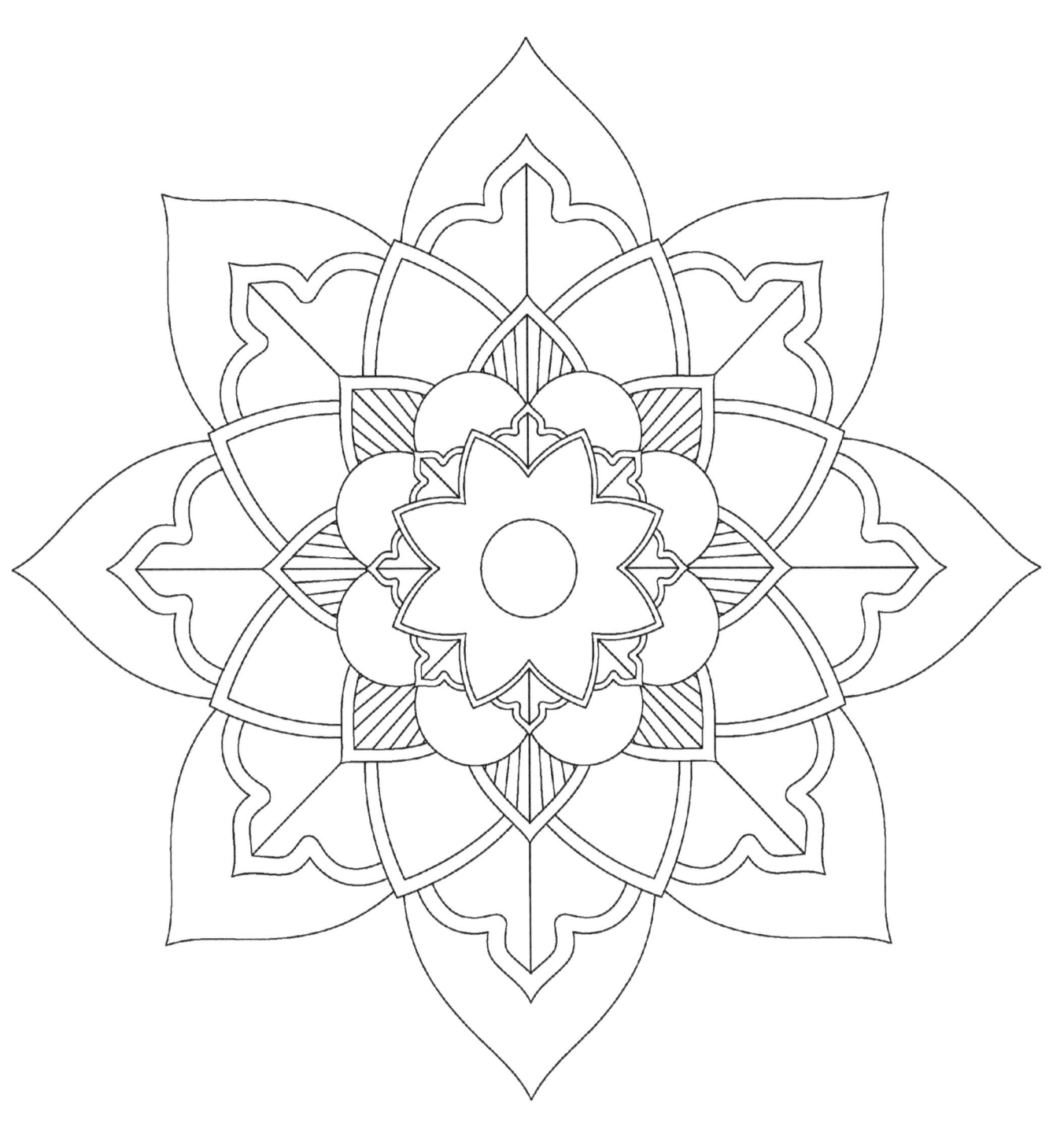

COLORS TEST

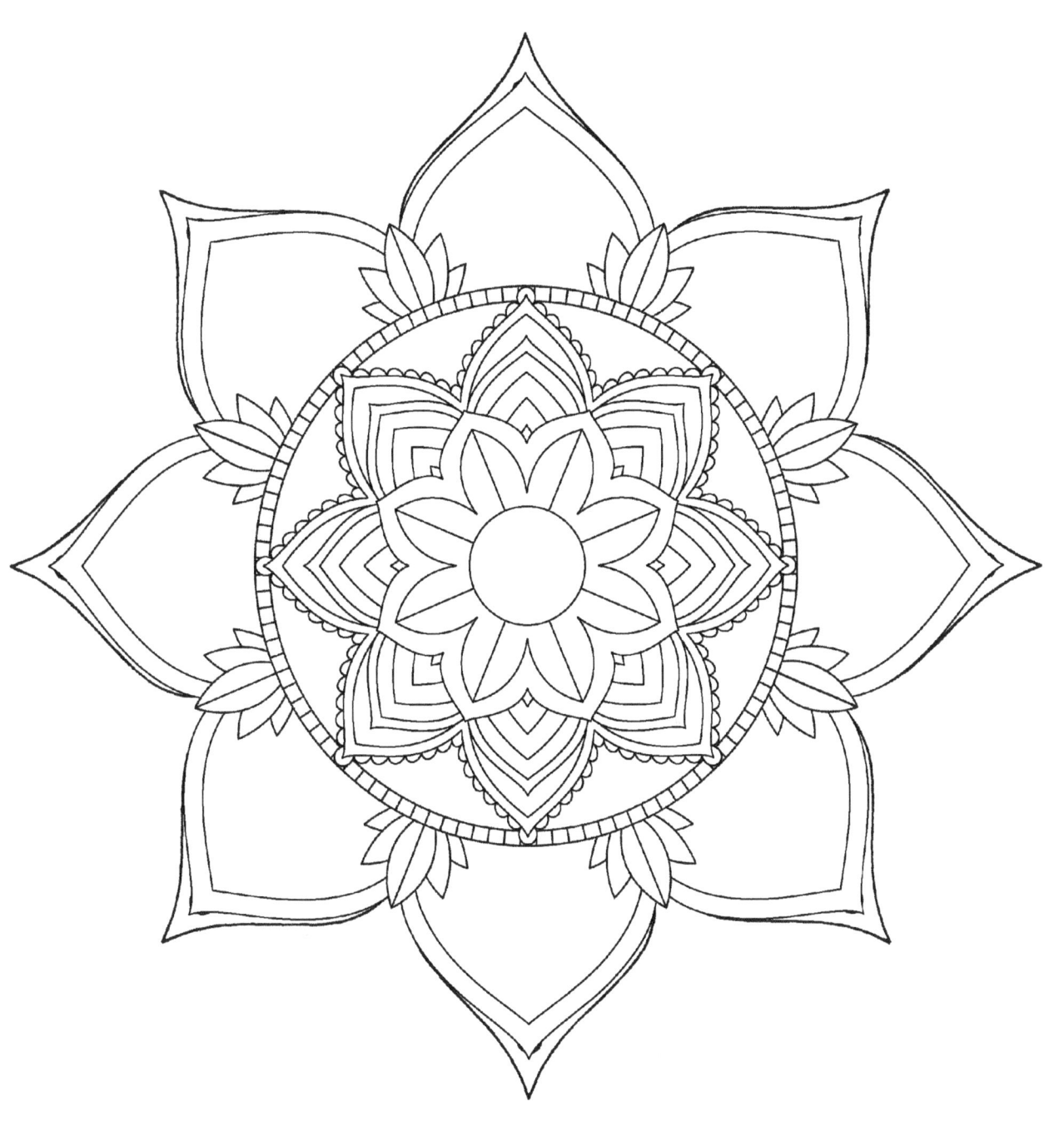

COLORS
TEST

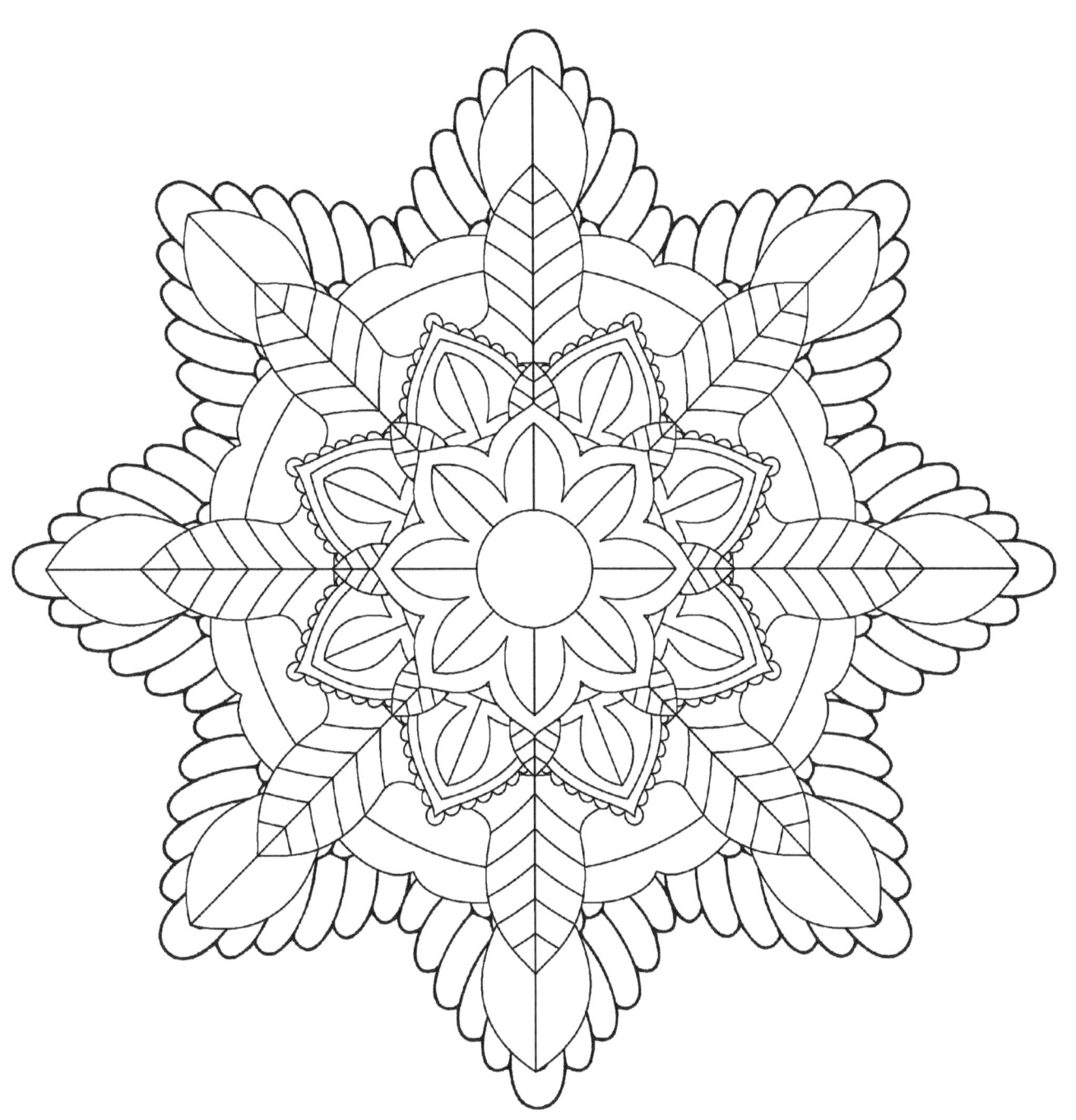

COLORS
TEST

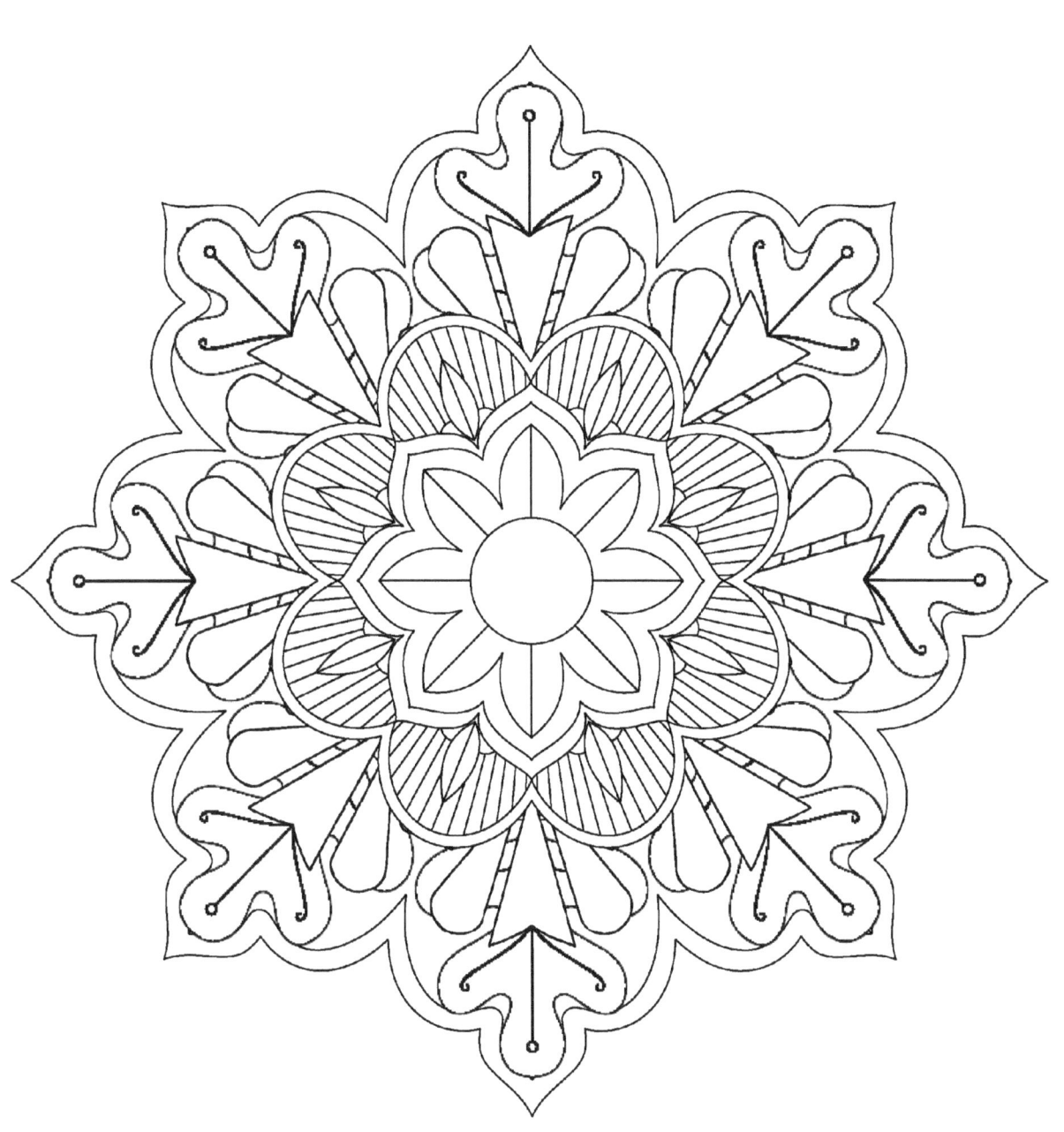

COLORS
TEST

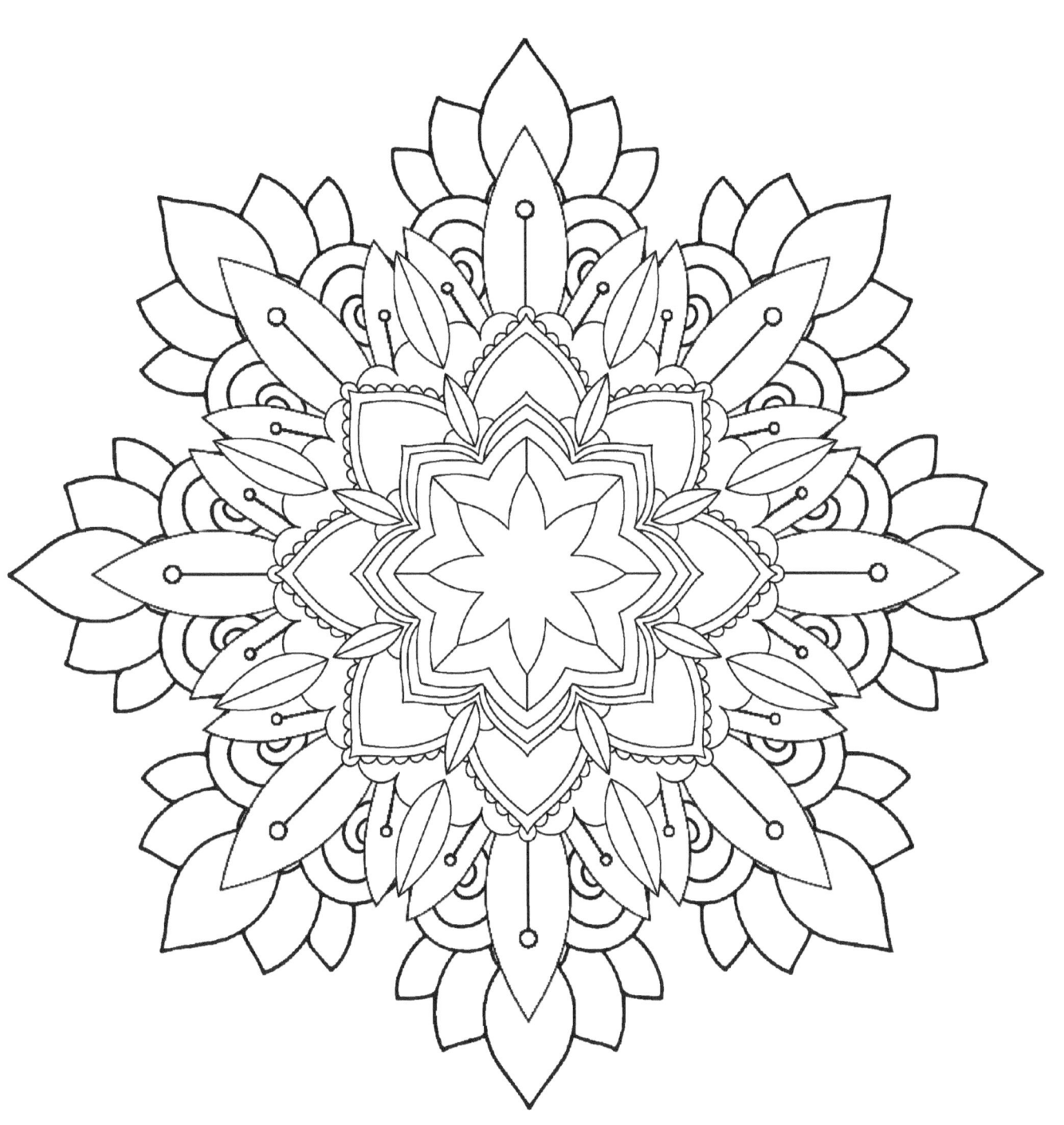

COLORS
TEST

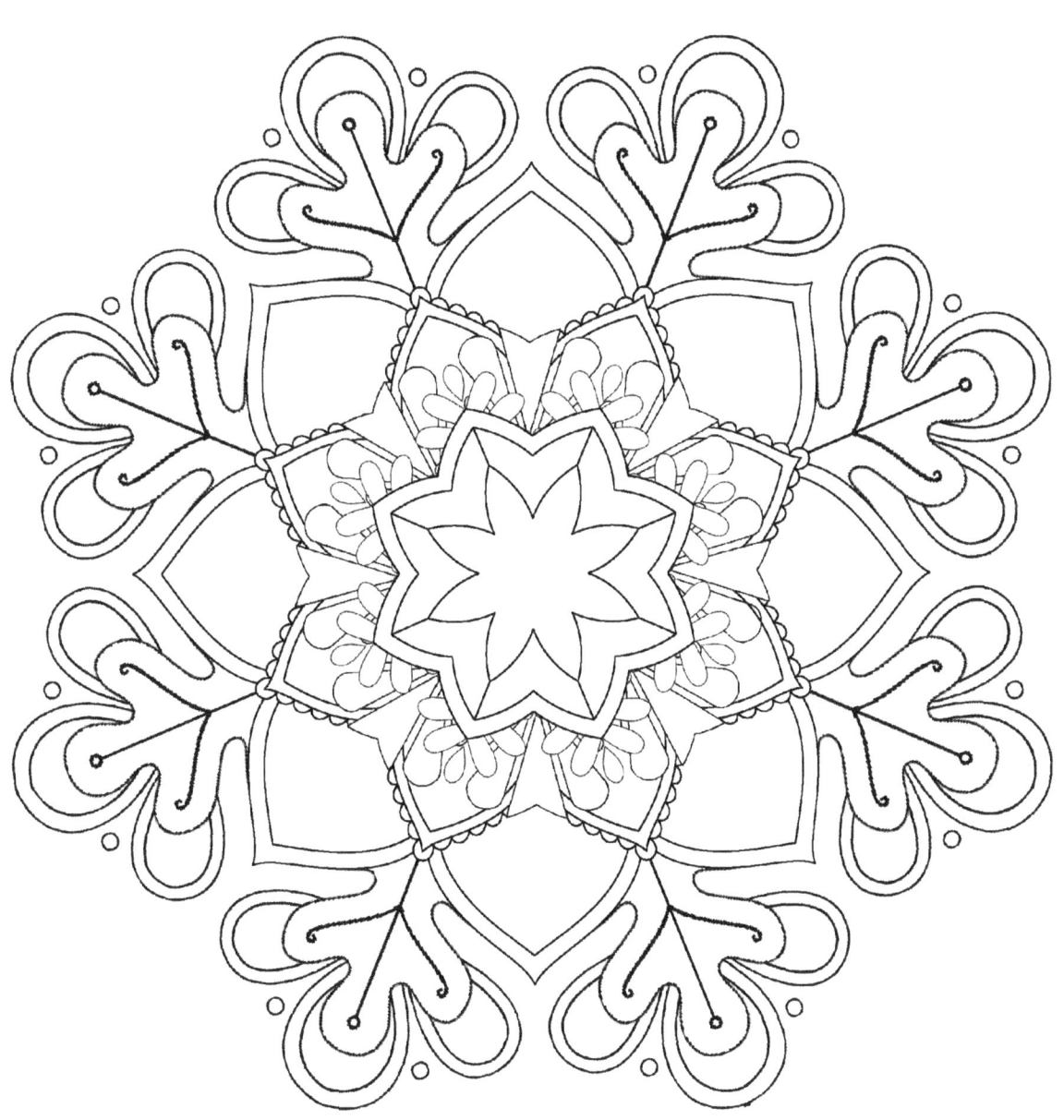

COLORS TEST

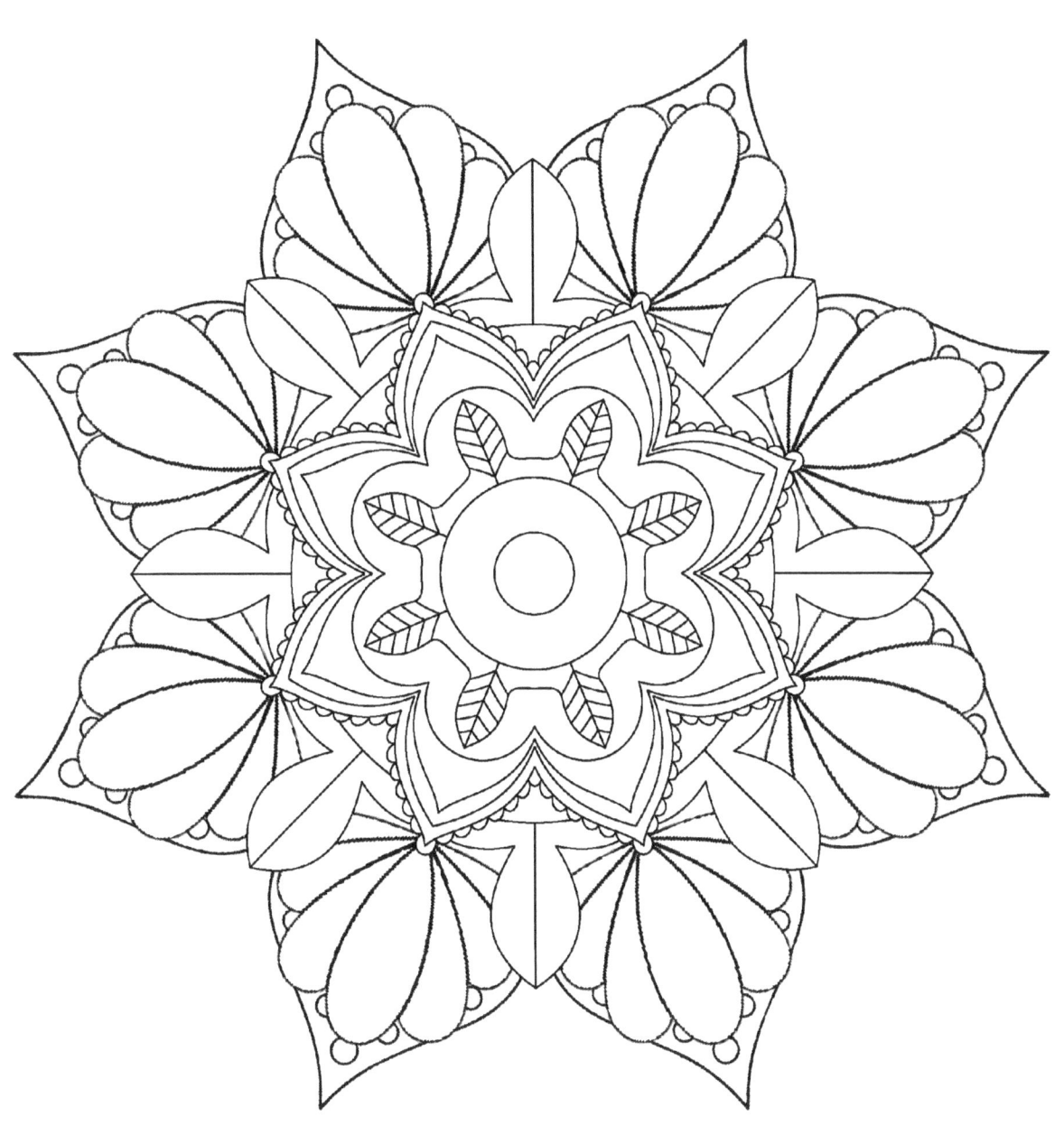

COLORS
TEST

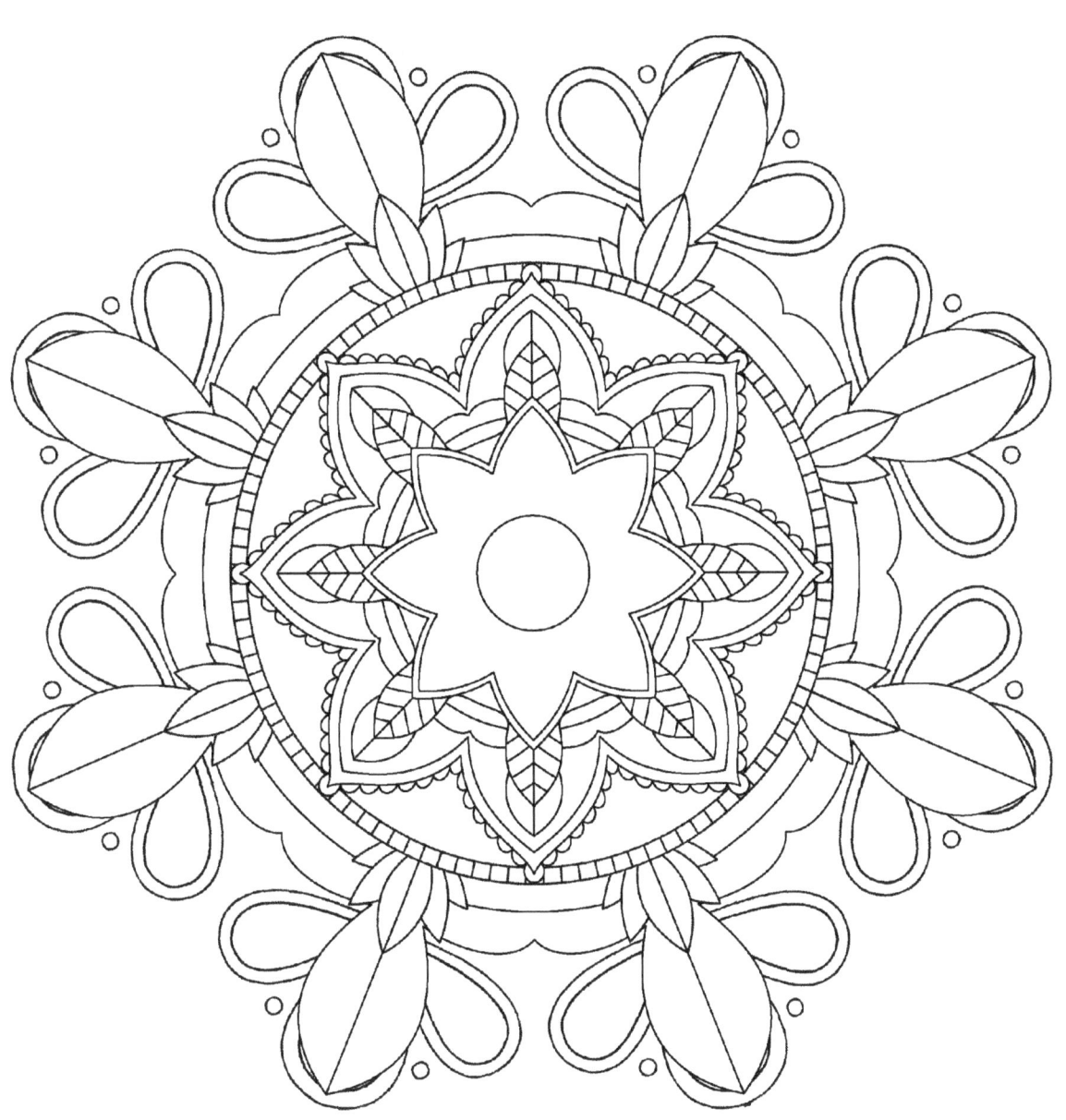

COLORS
TEST

COLORS
TEST

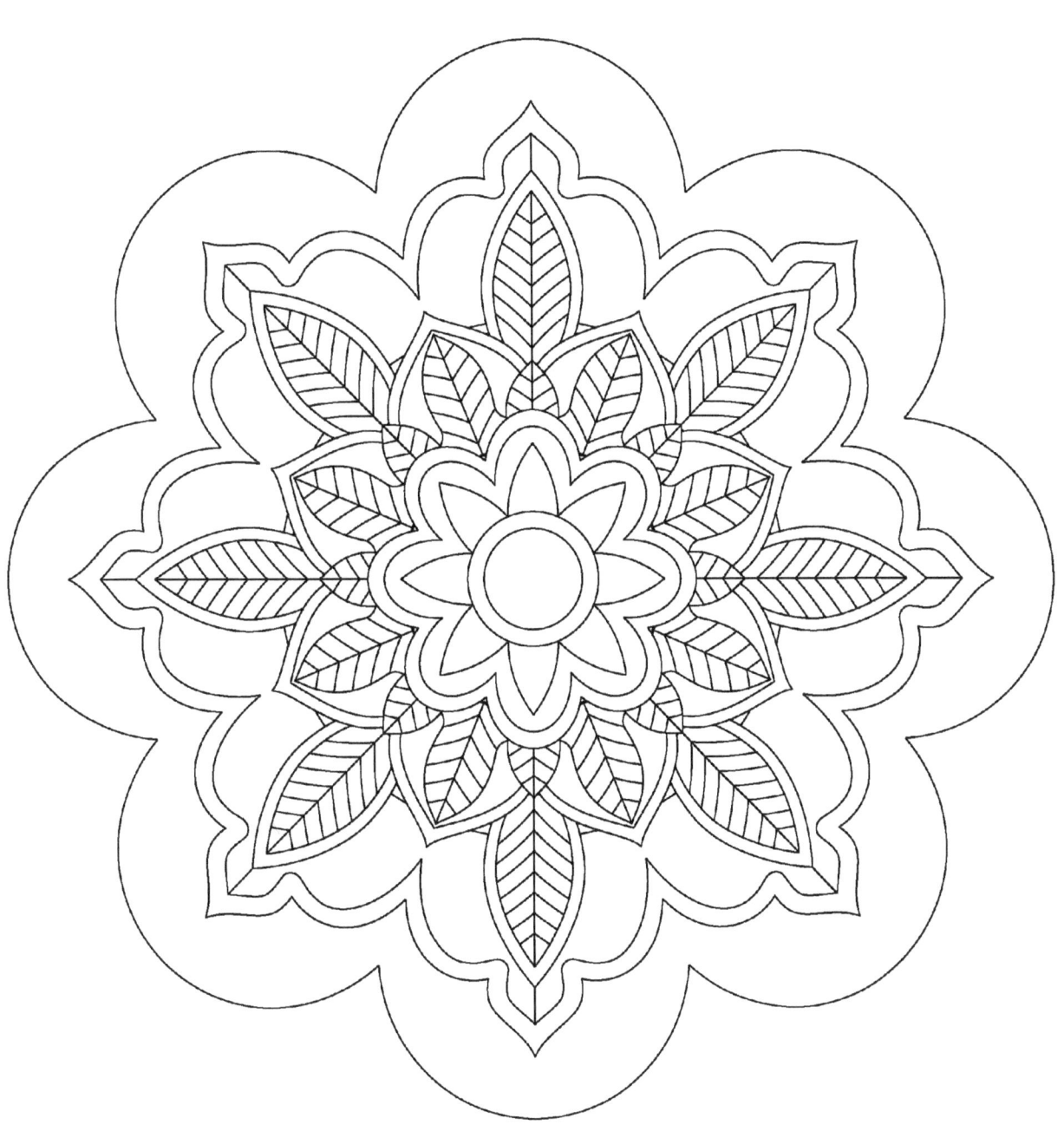

COLORS TEST

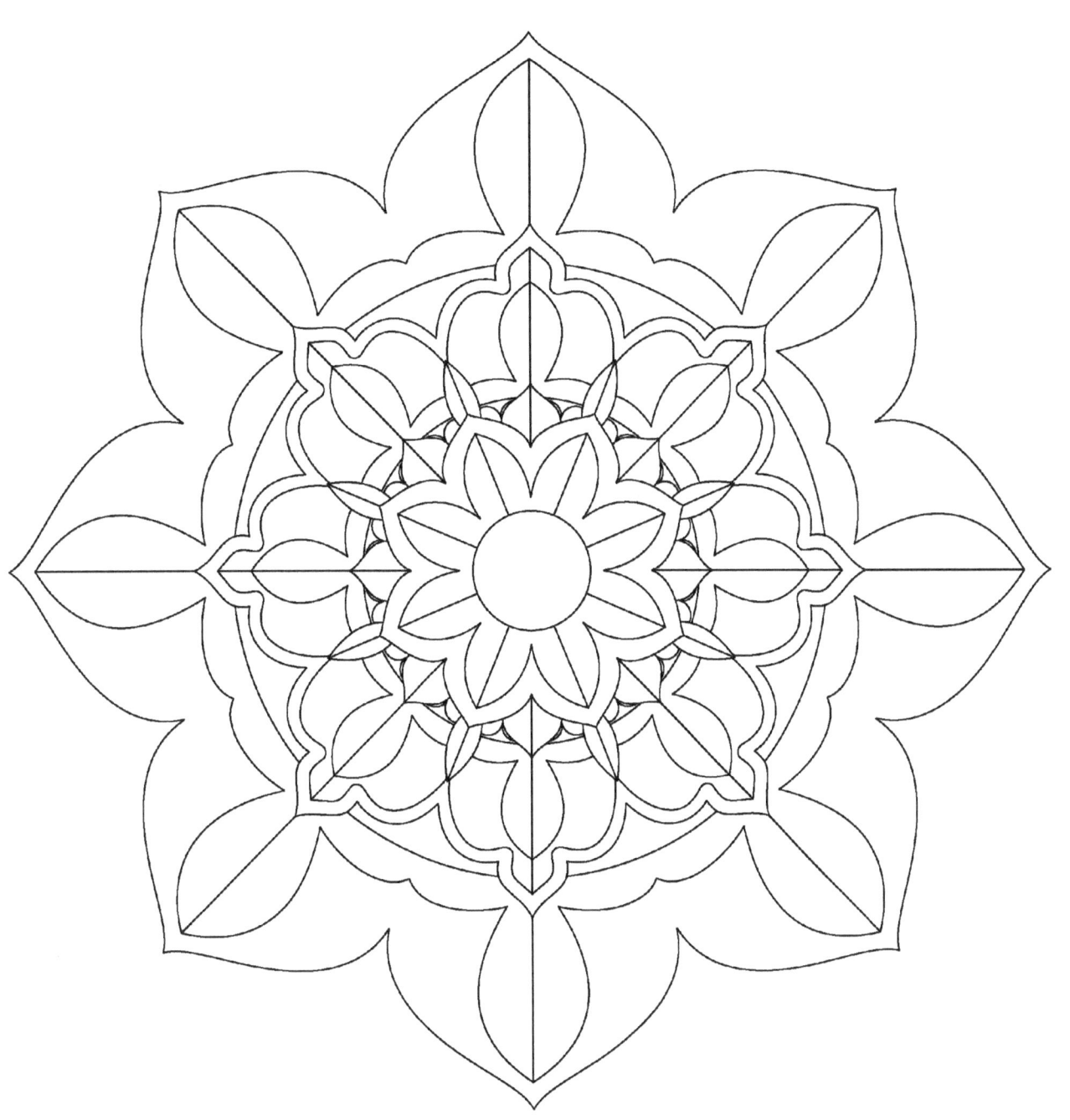

COLORS
TEST

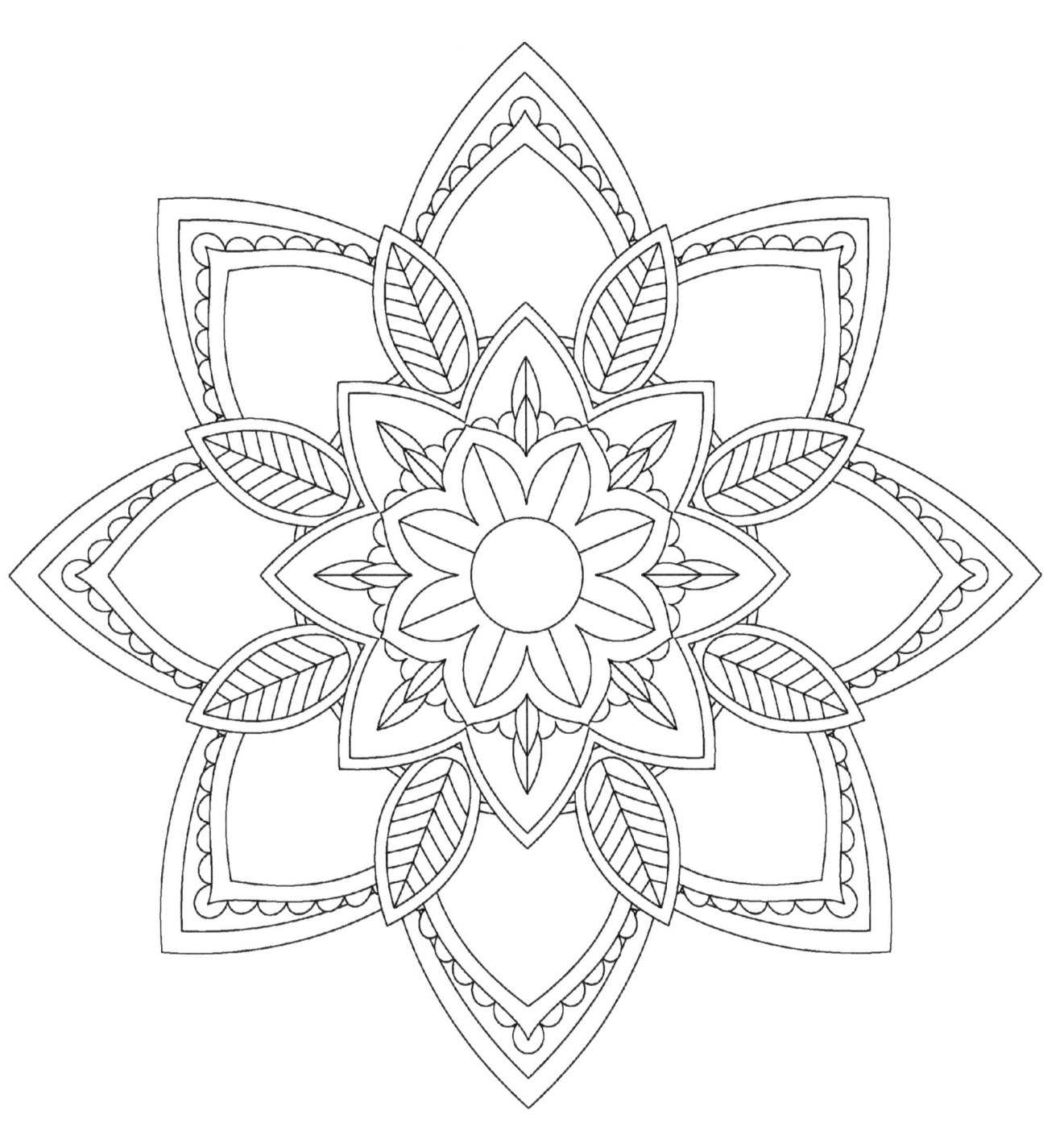

COLORS
TEST

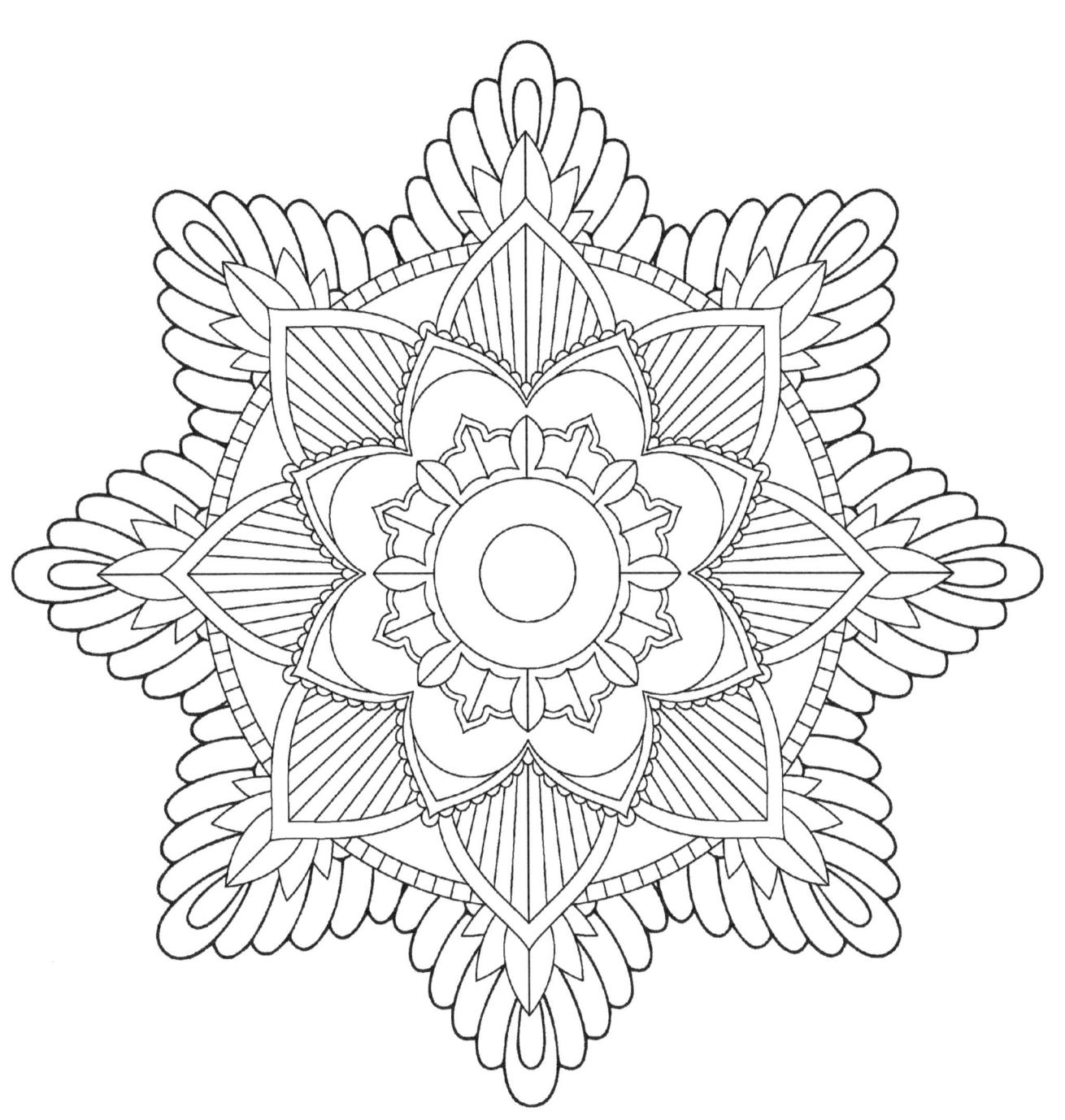

COLORS TEST

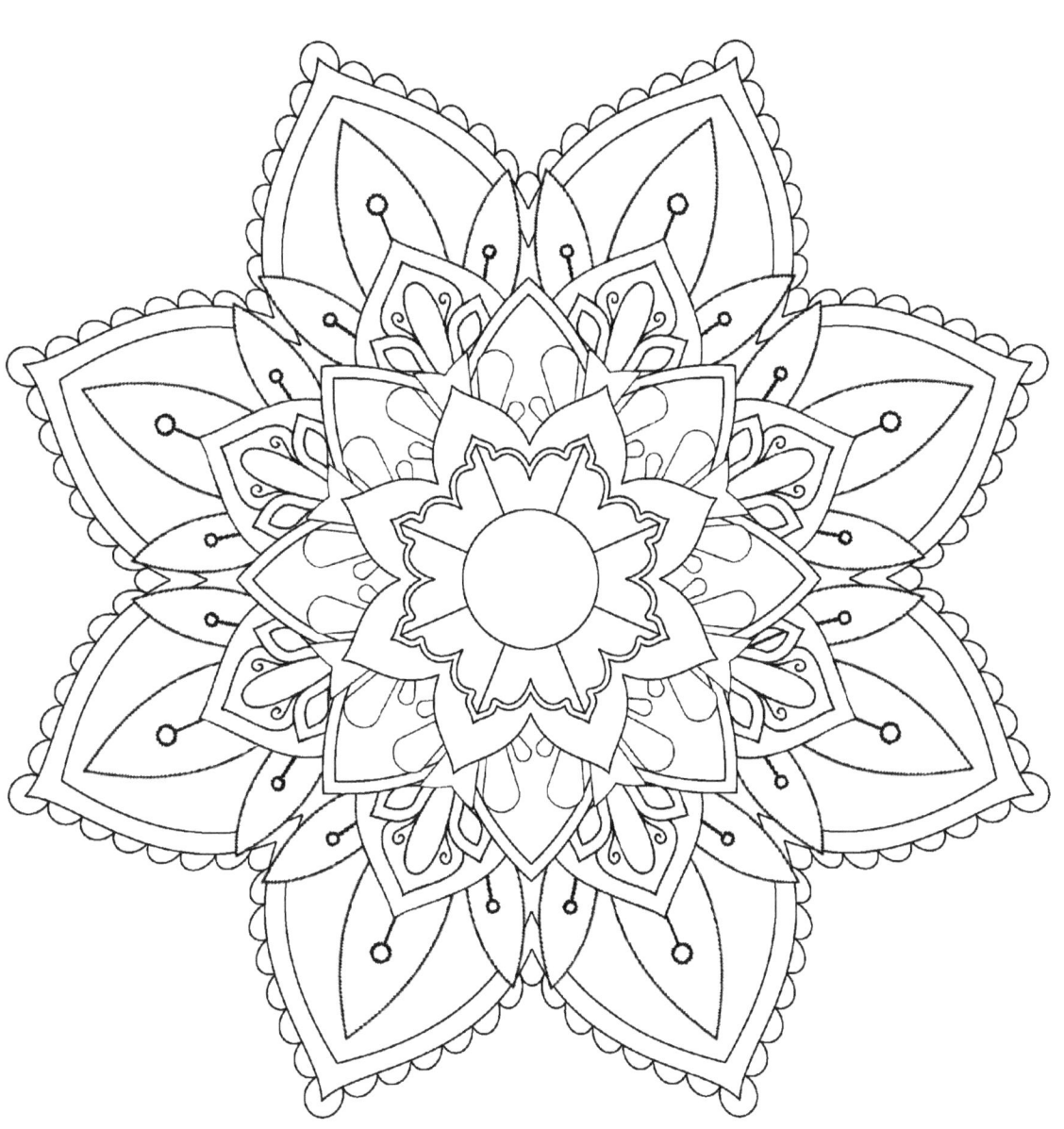

COLORS
TEST

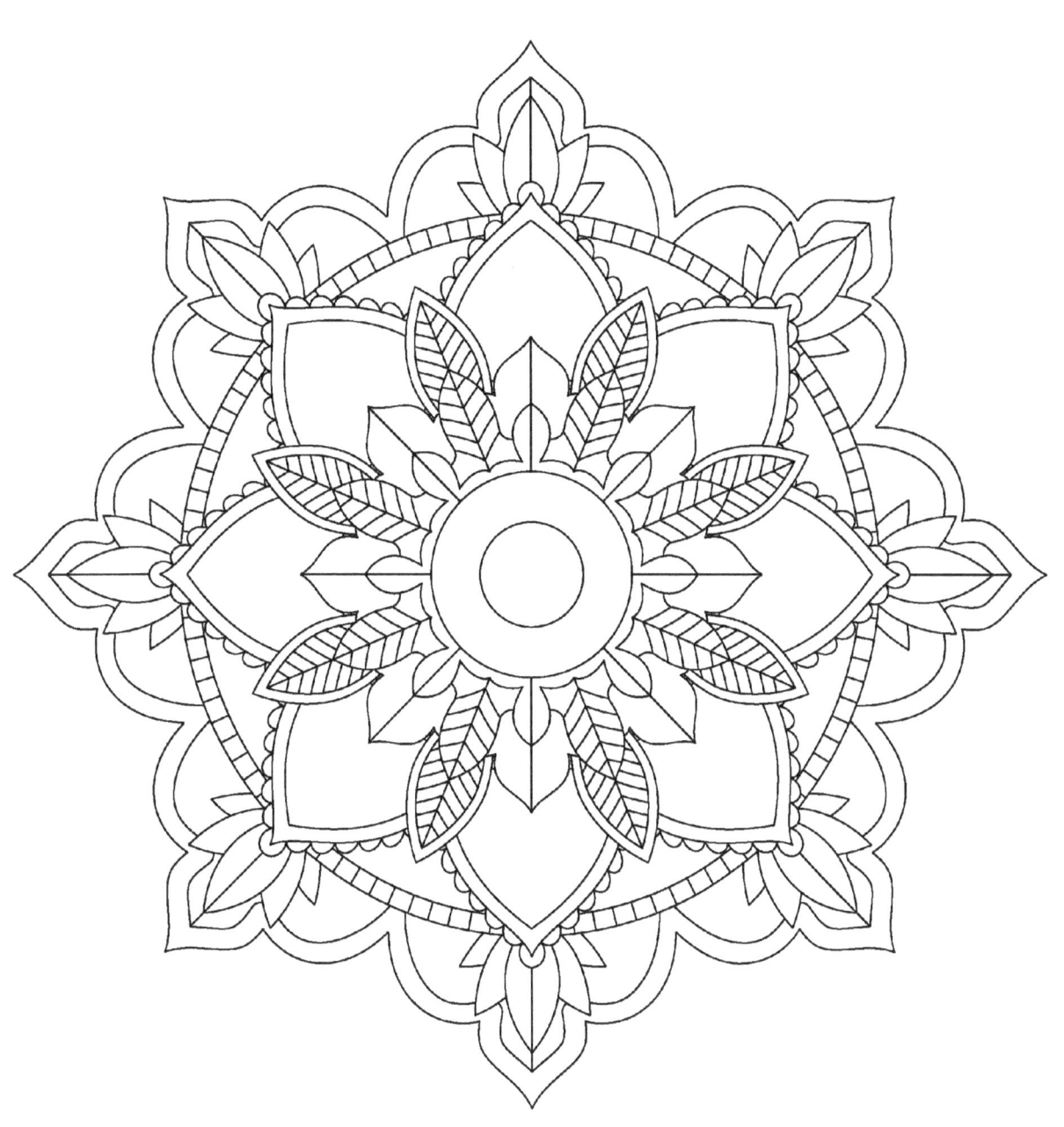

COLORS
TEST

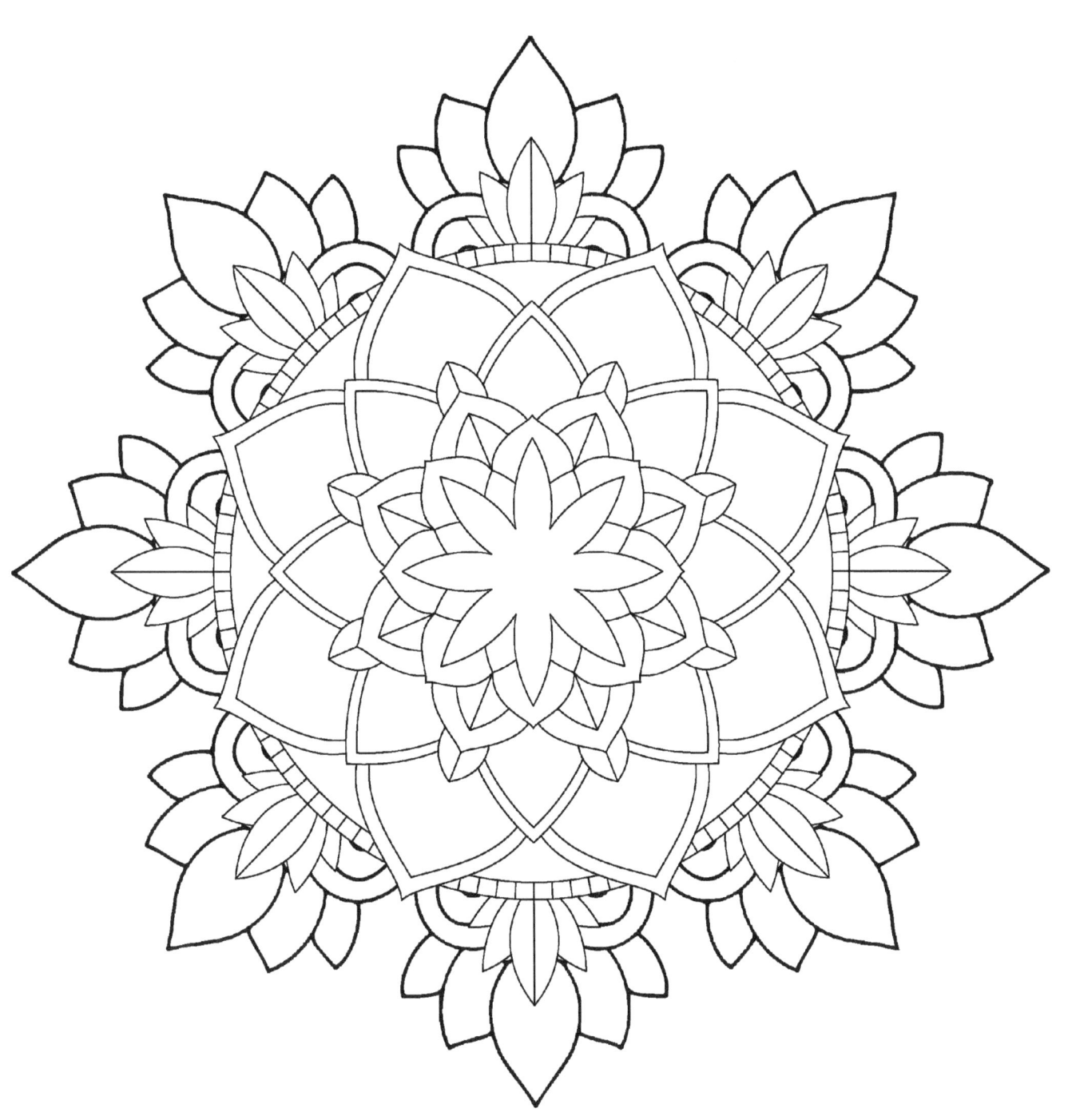

COLORS TEST

COLORS
TEST

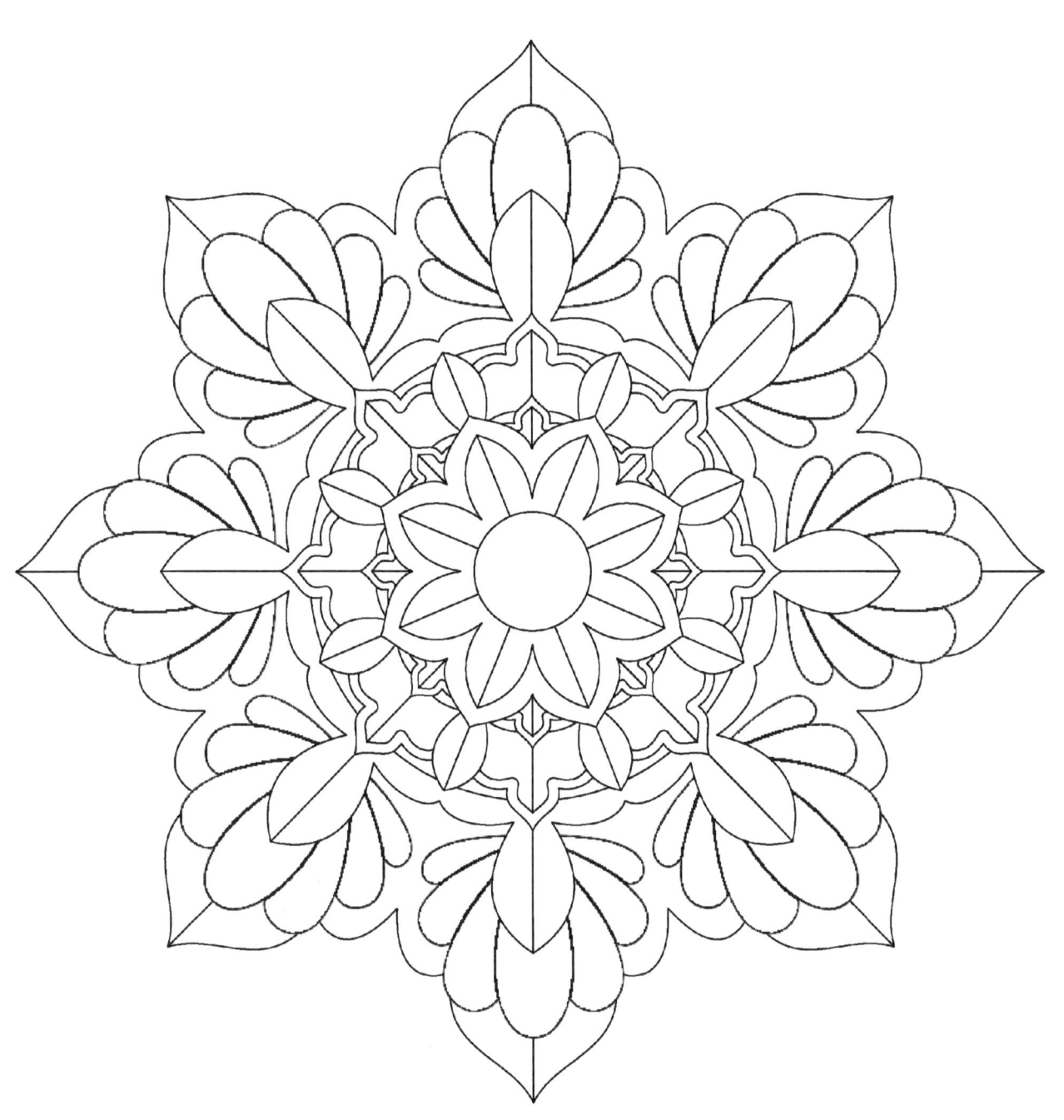

COLORS
TEST

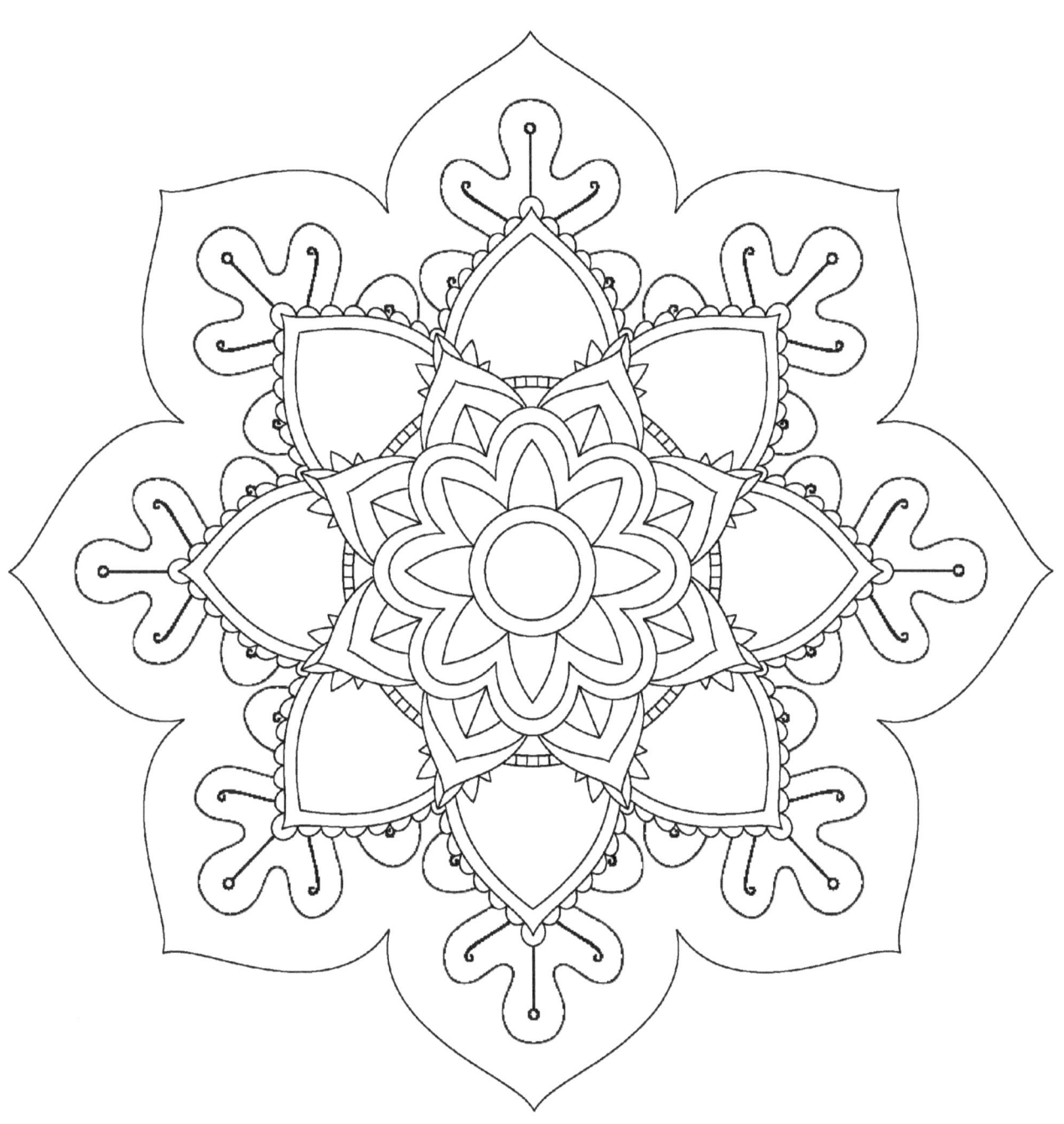

COLORS TEST

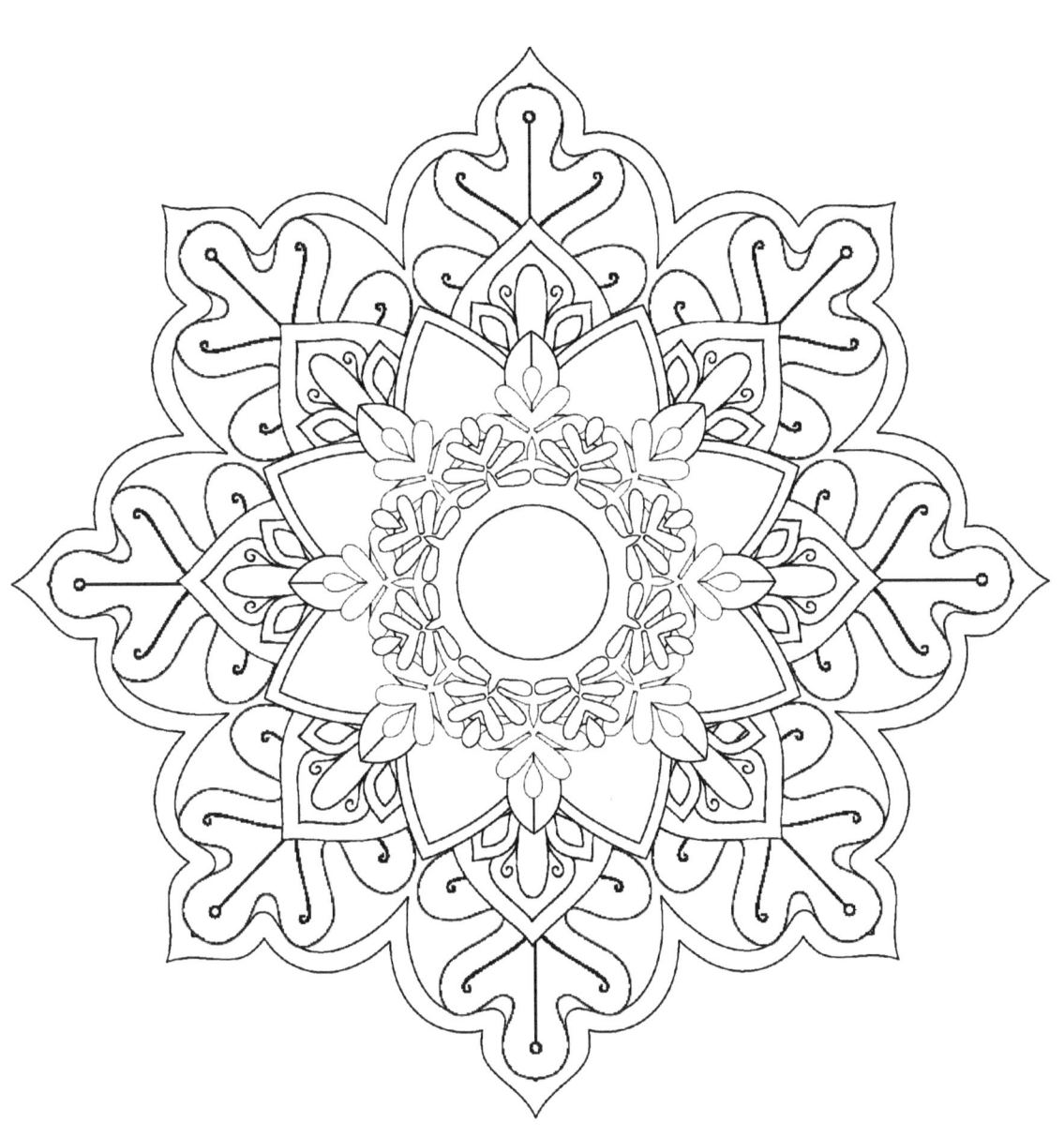

COLORS TEST

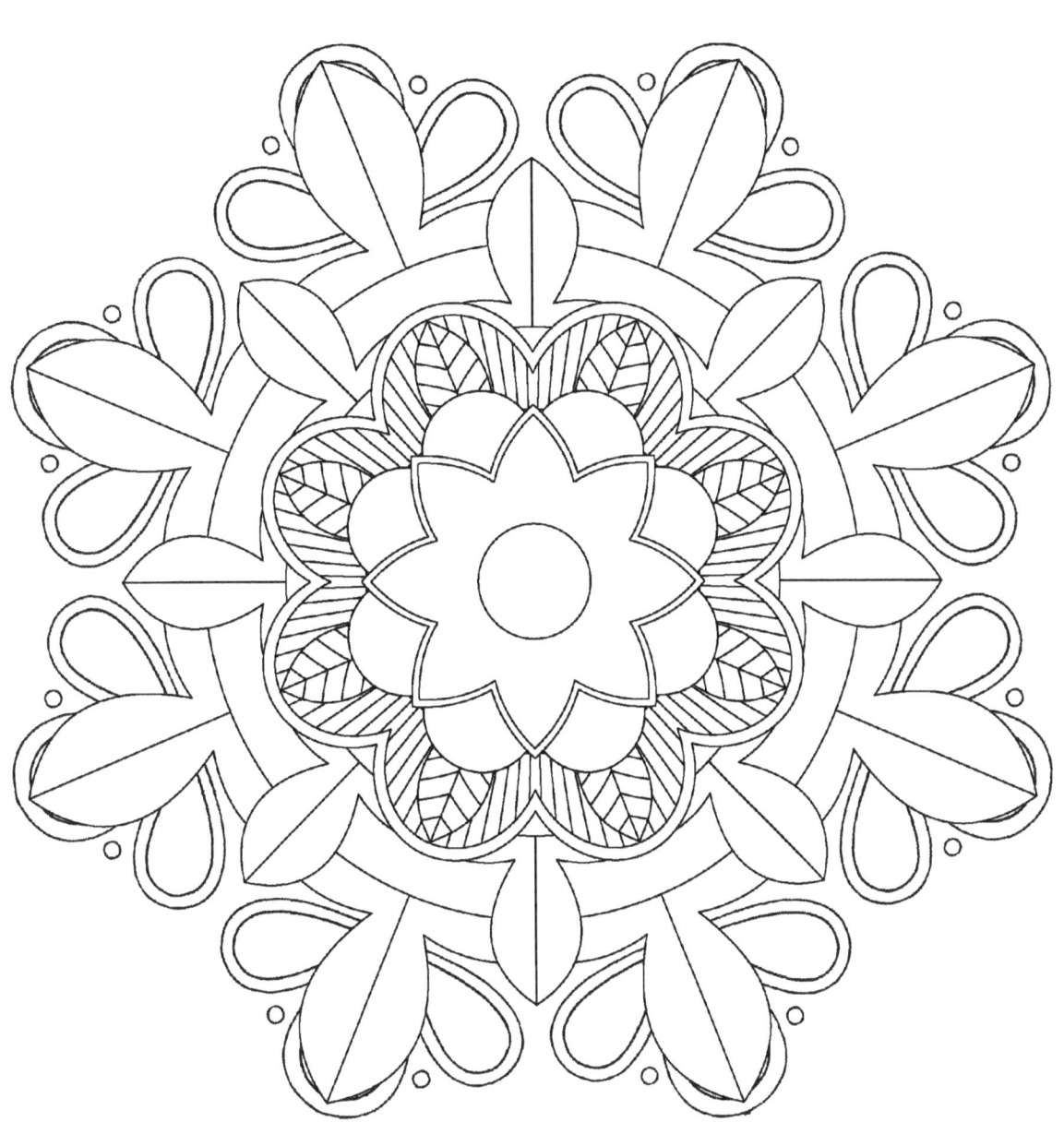

COLORS
TEST

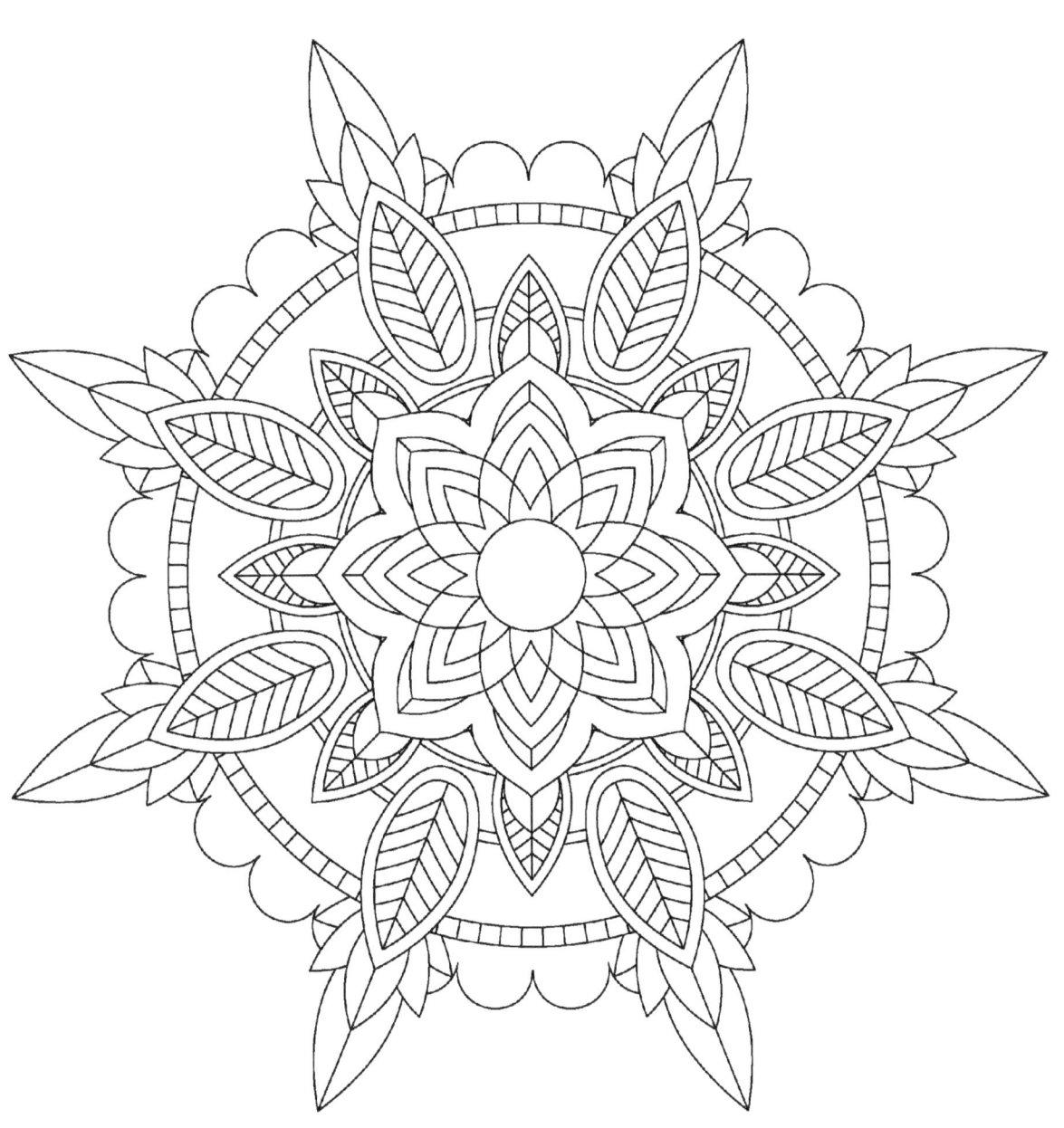

COLORS
TEST

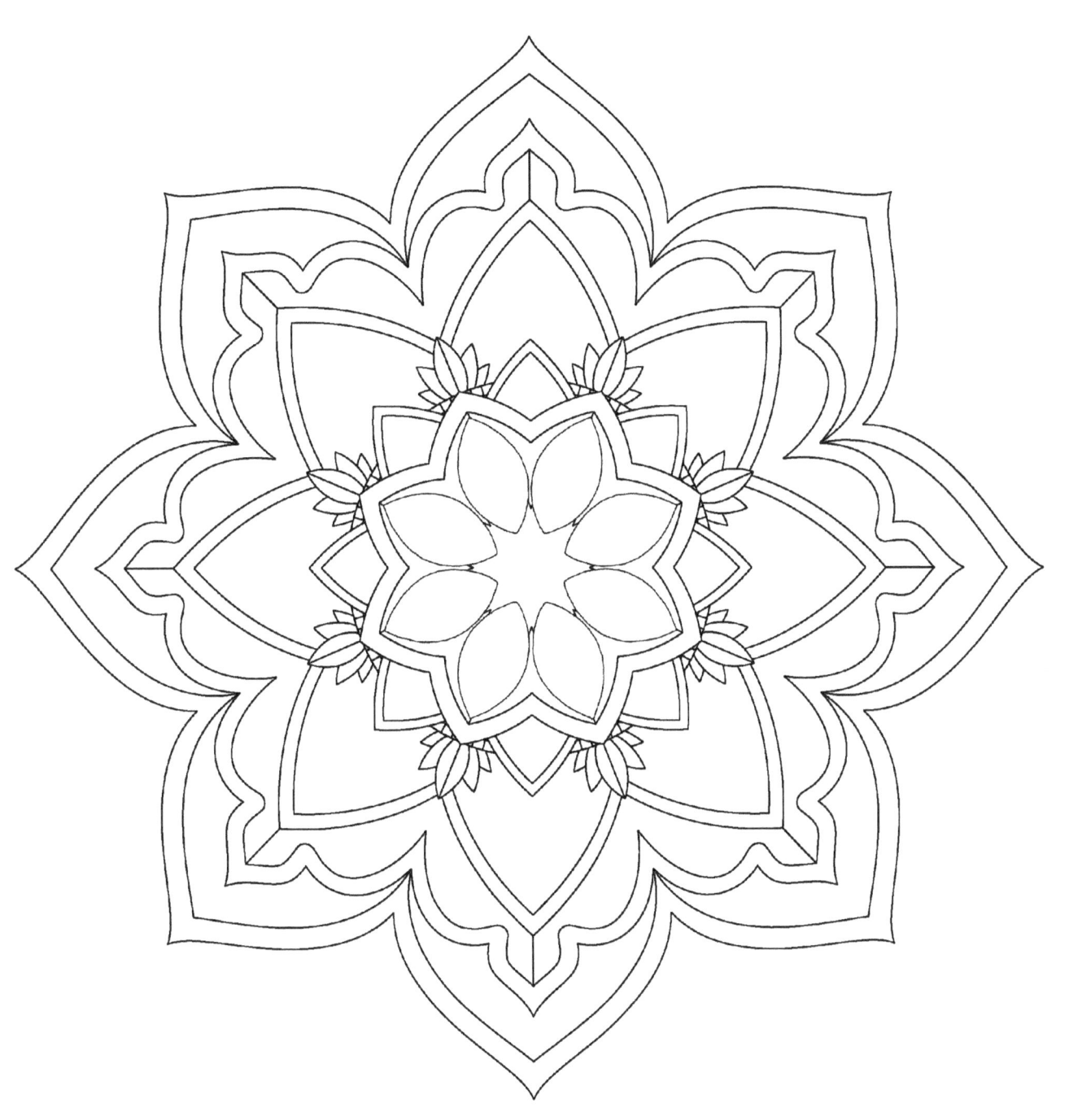

COLORS TEST

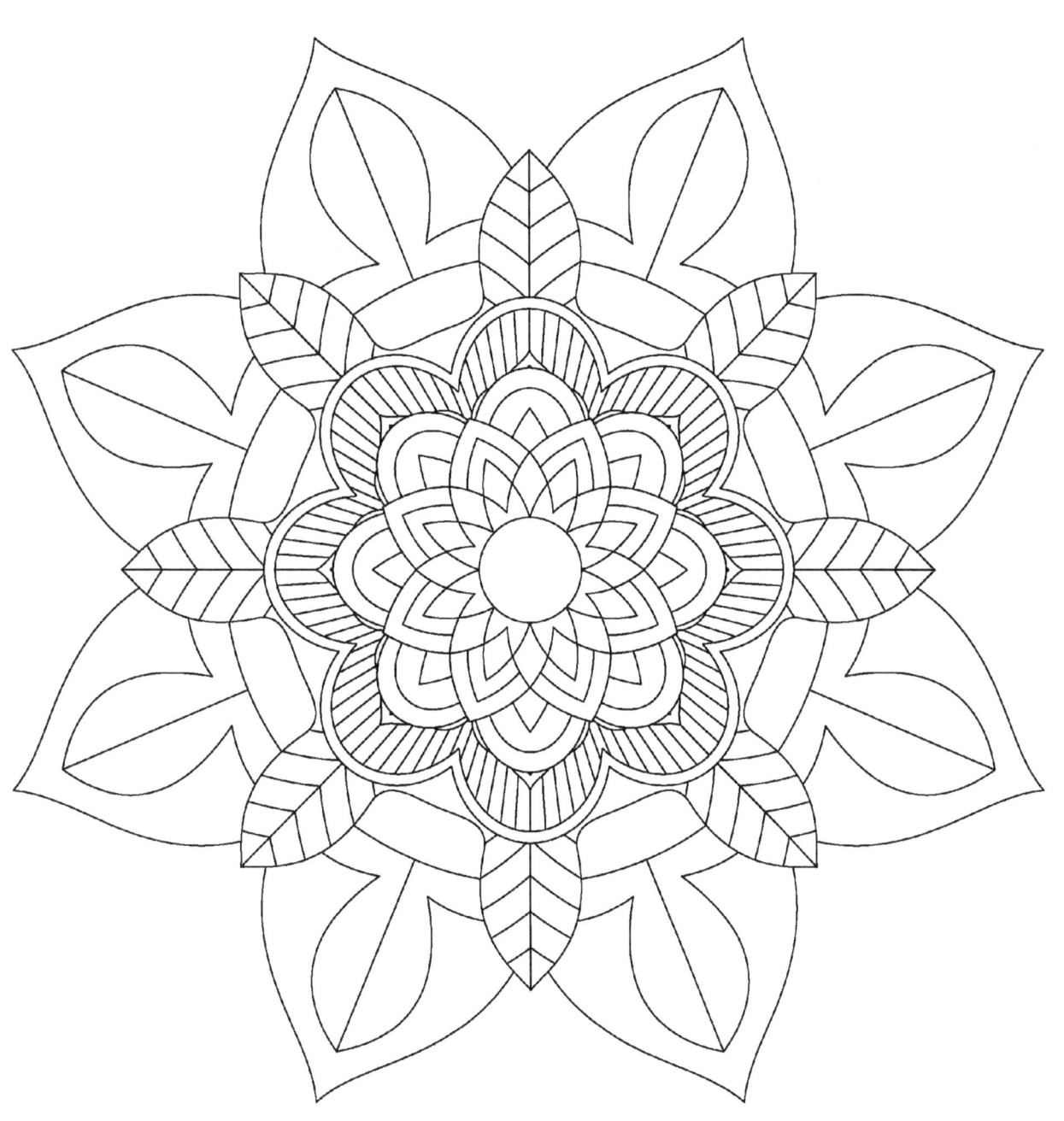

COLORS
TEST

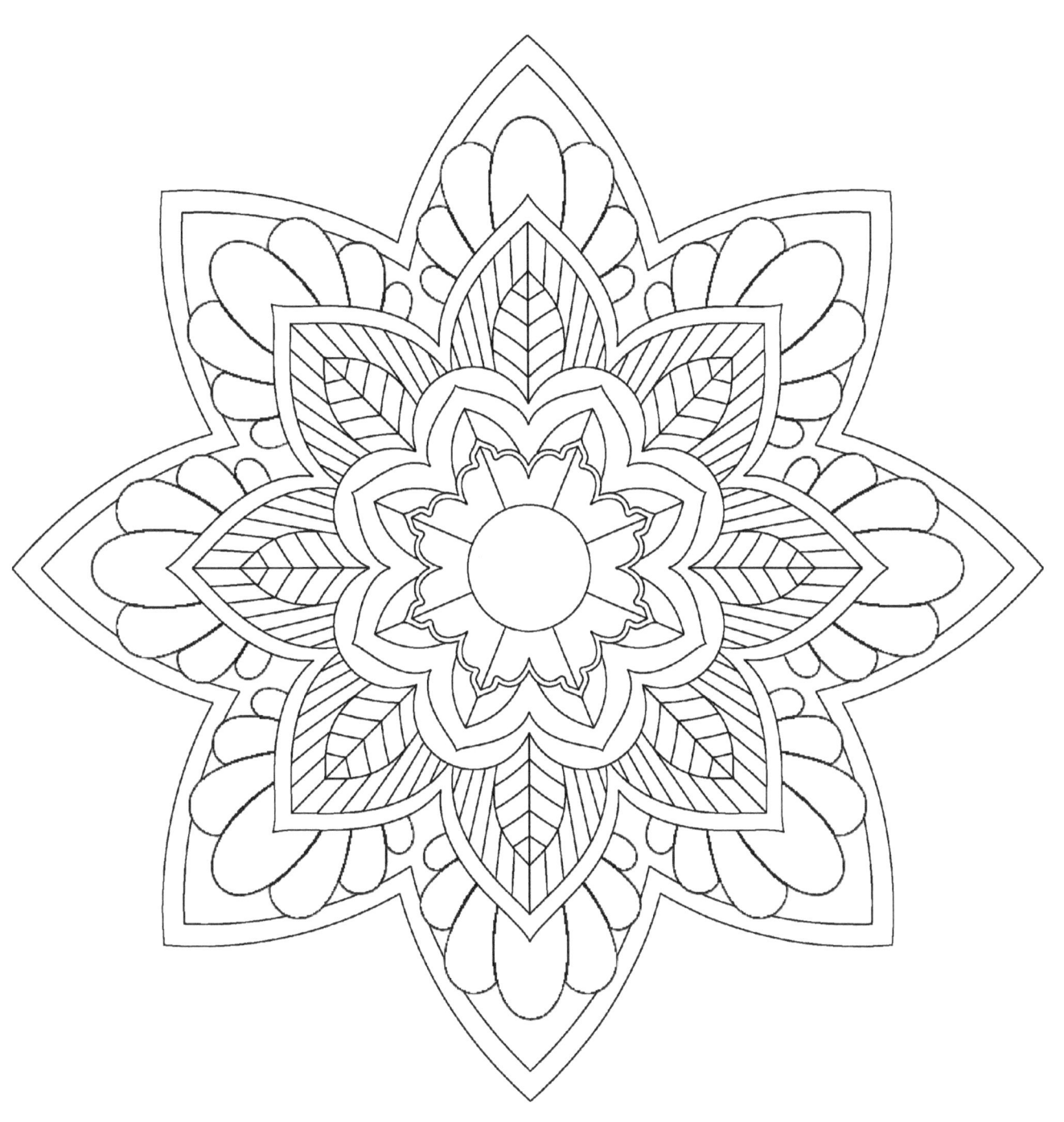

COLORS TEST

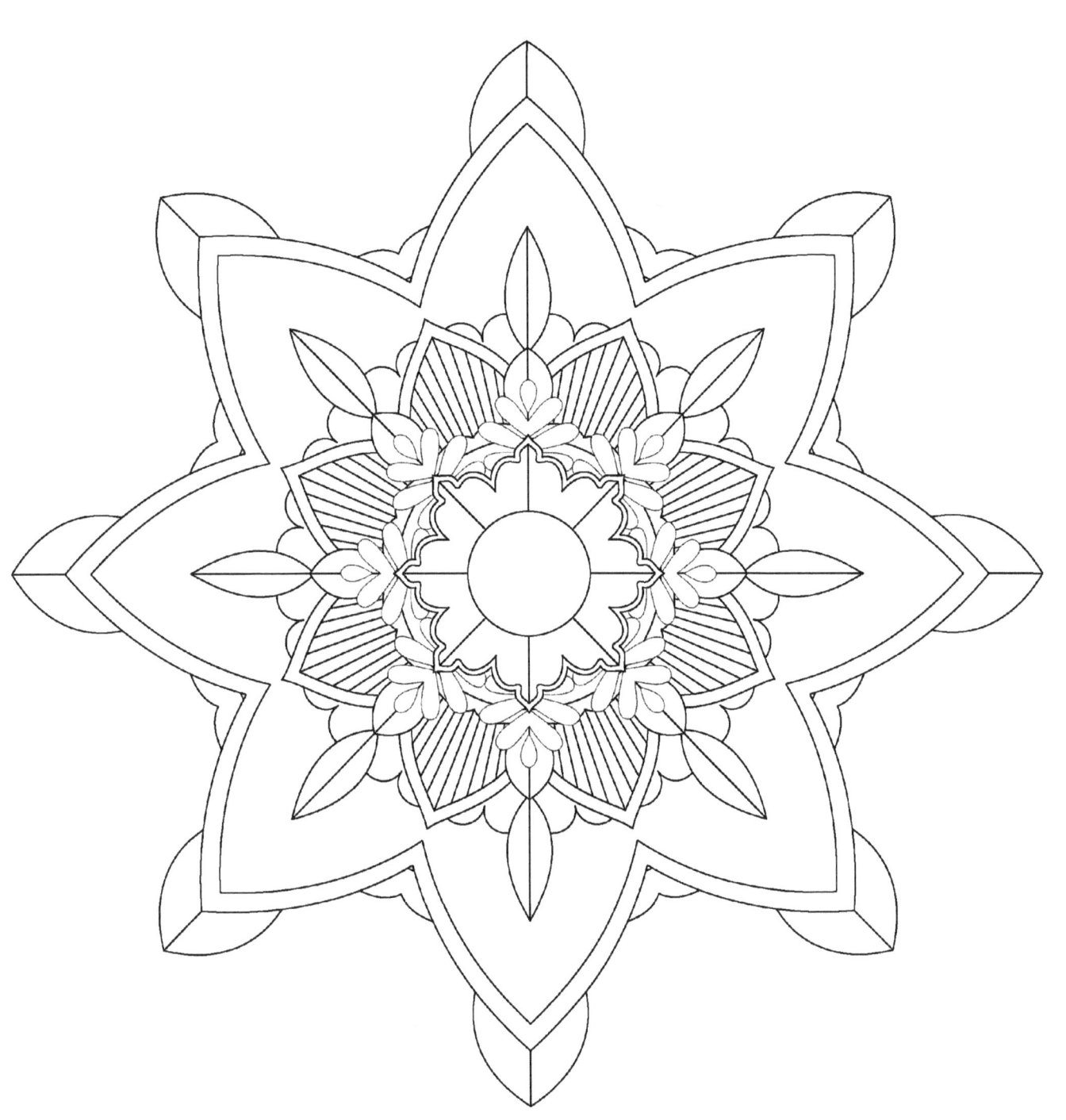

COLORS
TEST

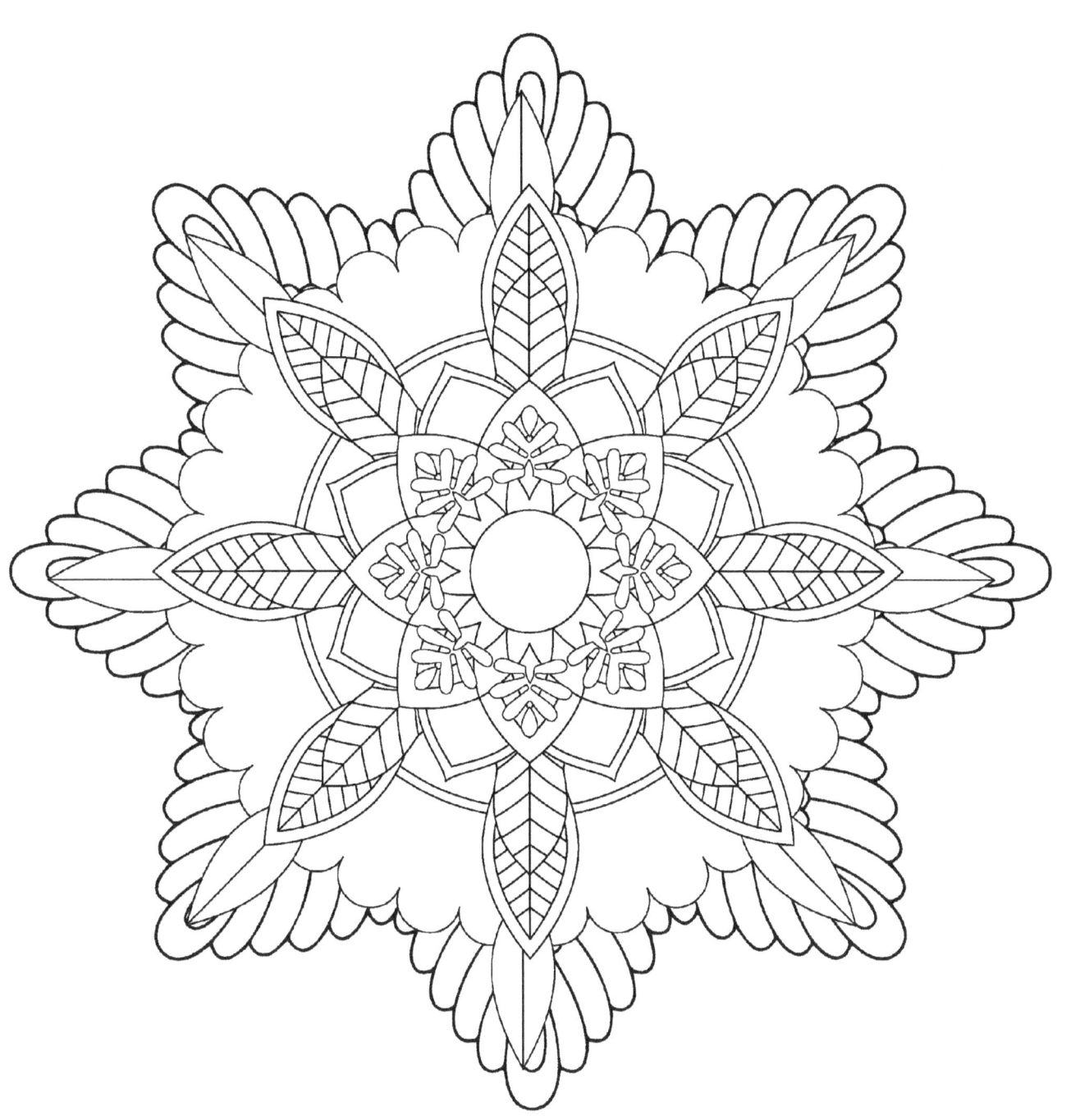

COLORS
TEST

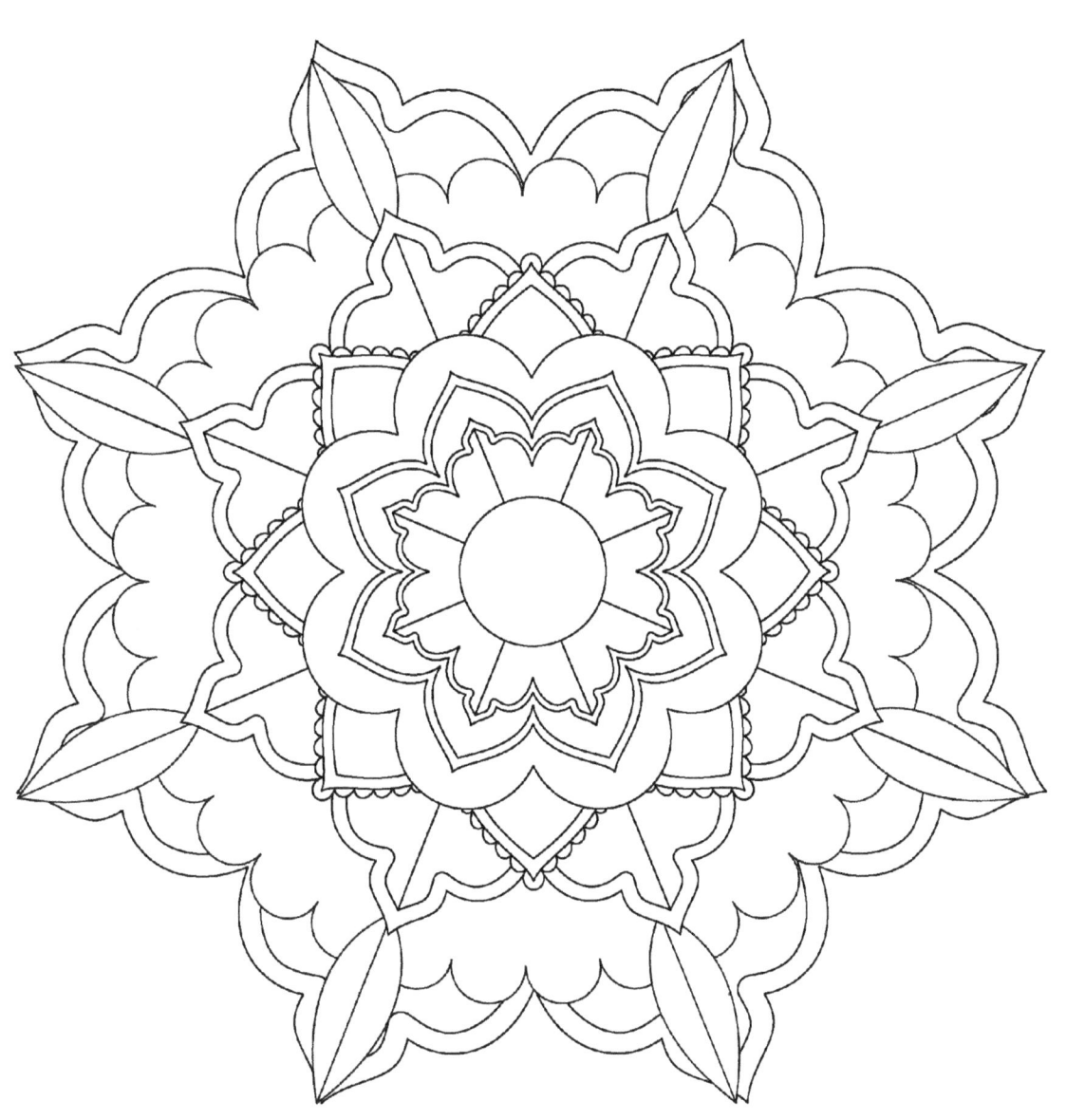

COLORS TEST

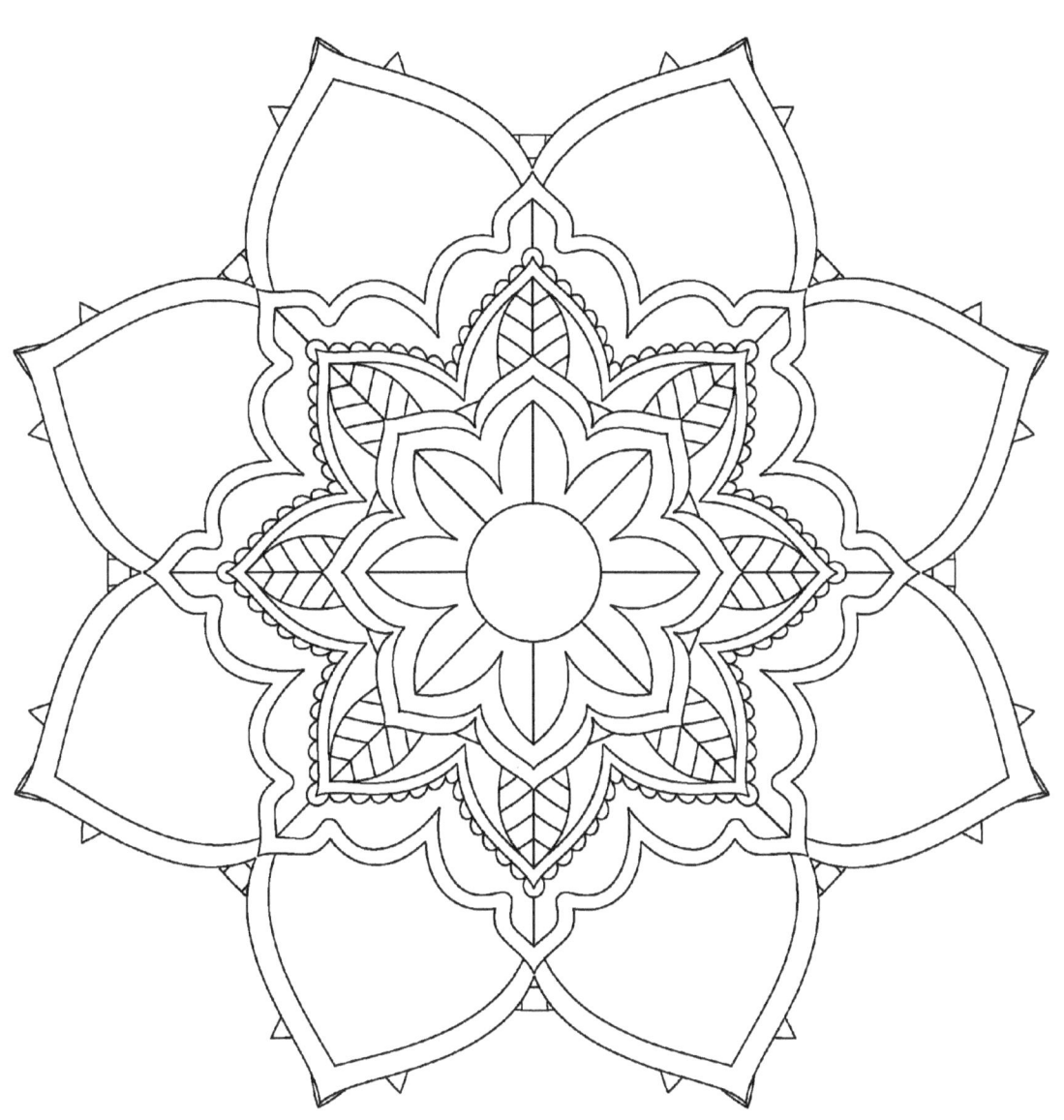

COLORS
TEST

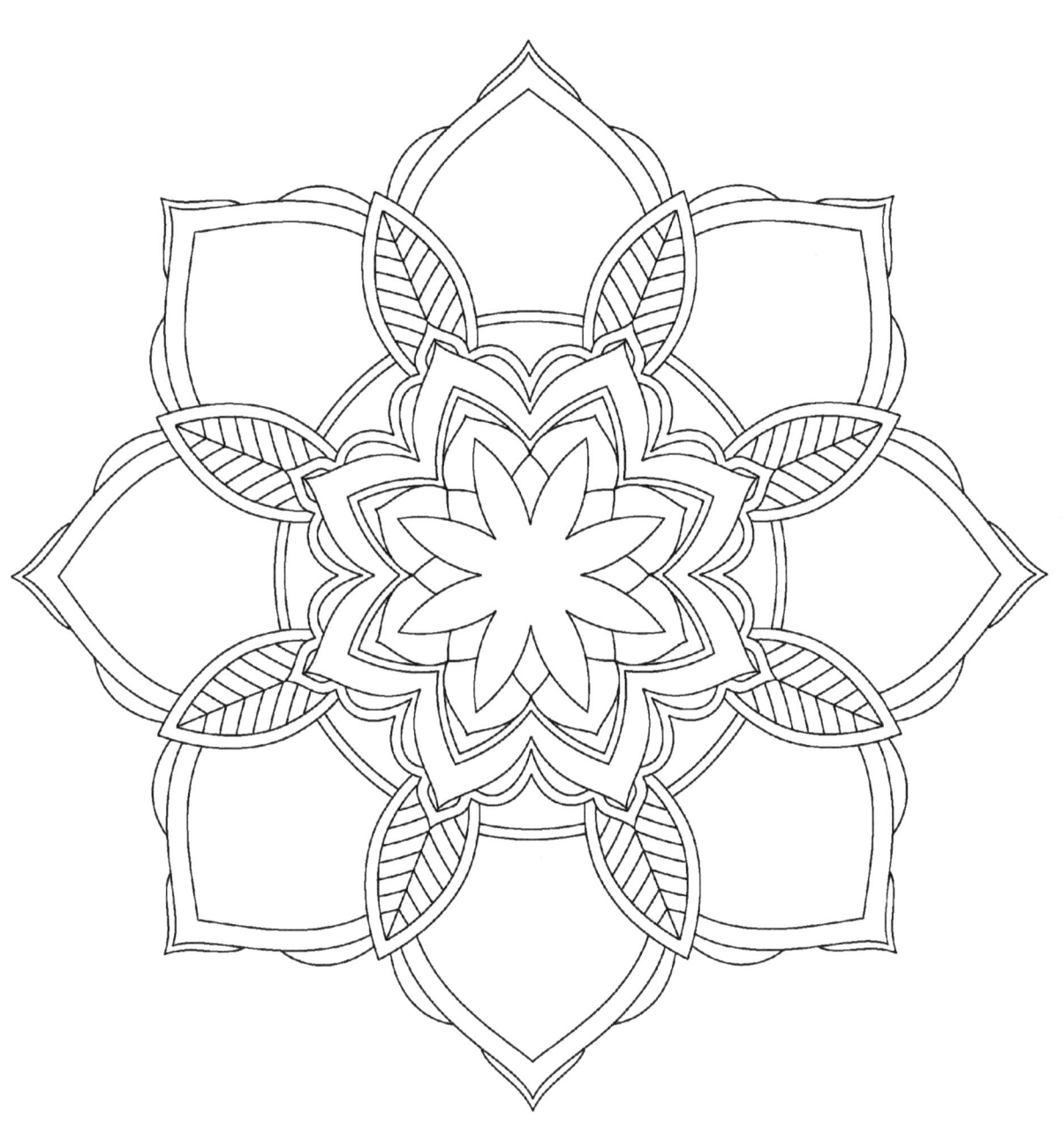

COLORS TEST

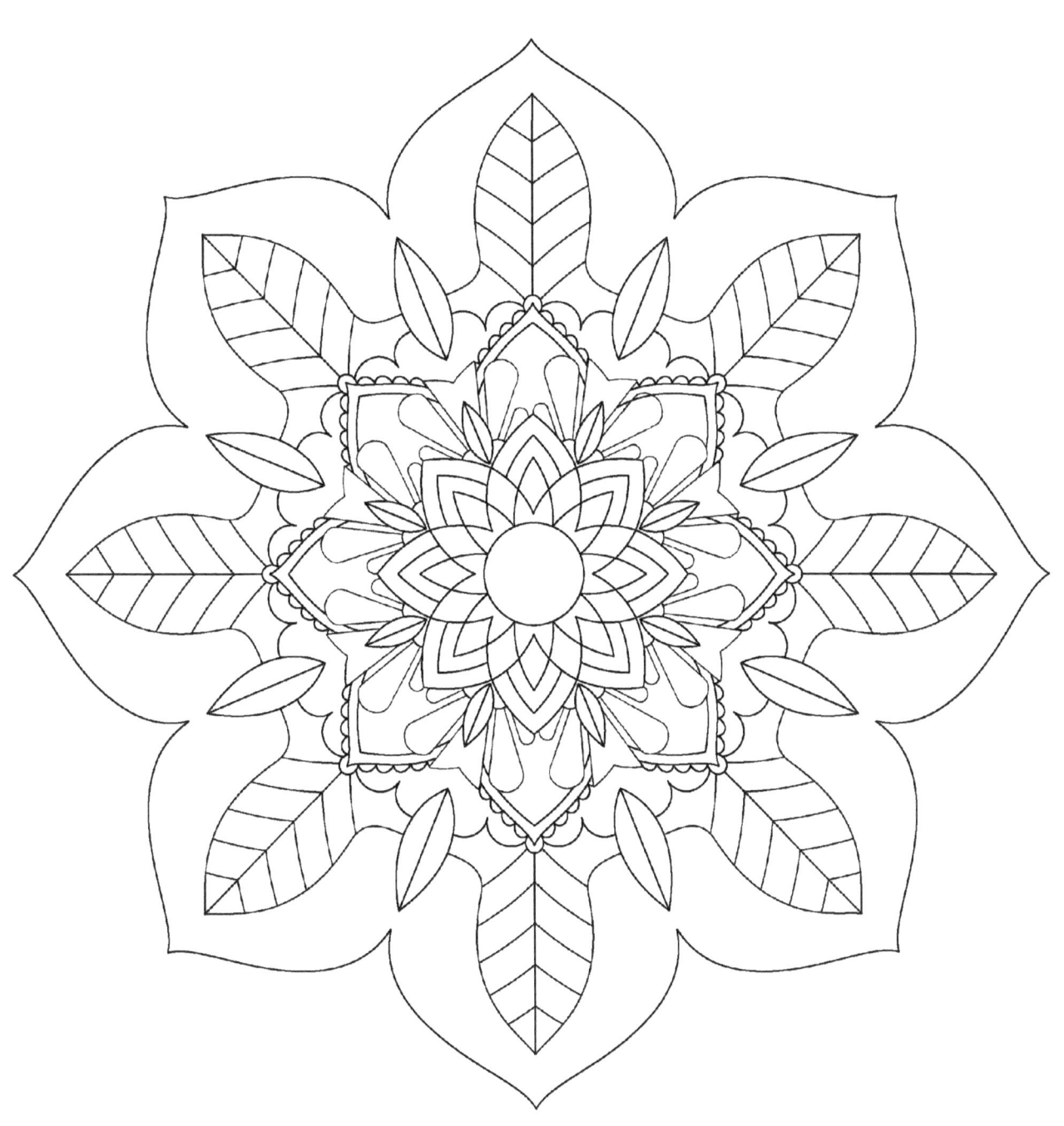

COLORS
TEST

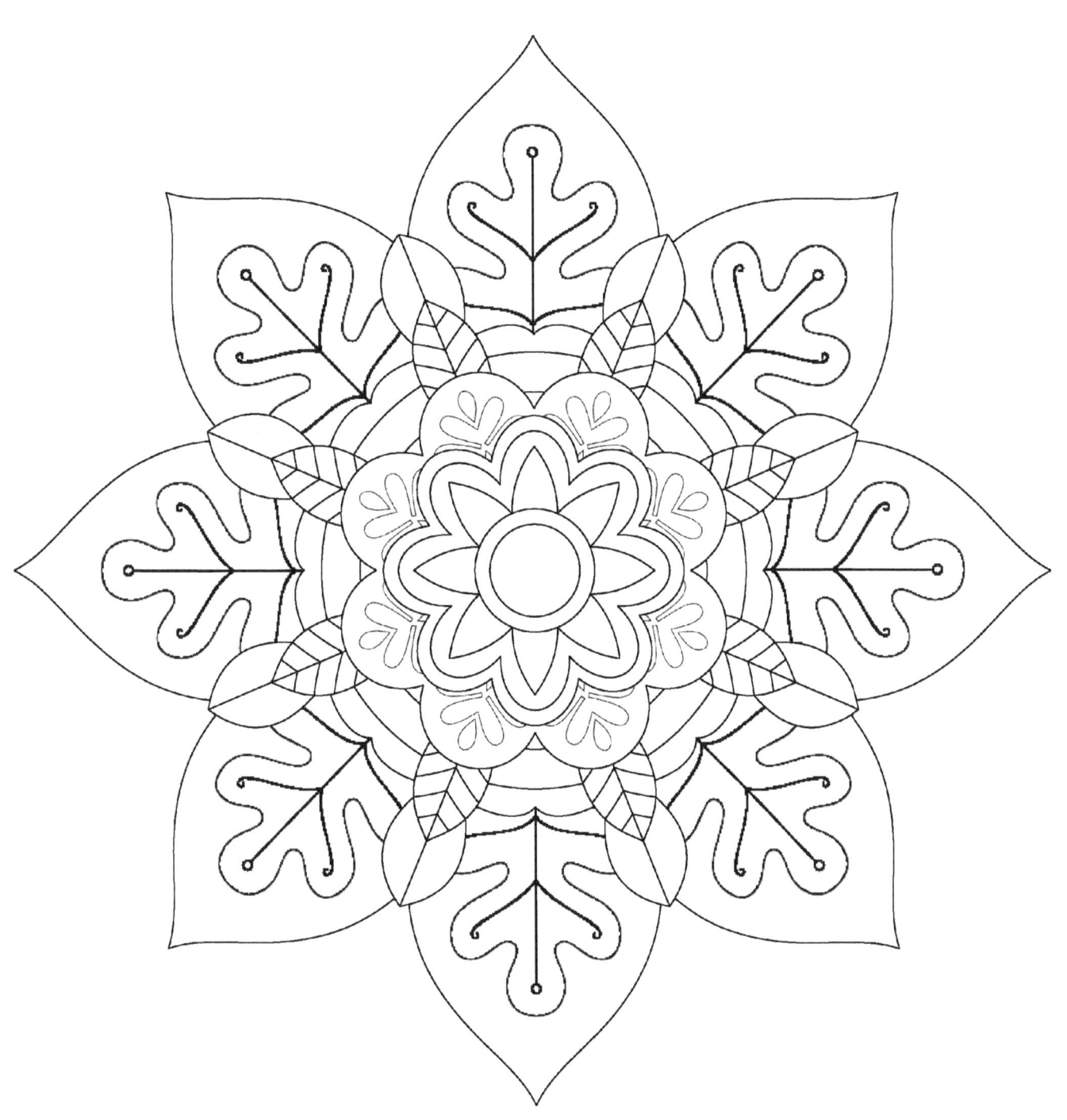

COLORS
TEST

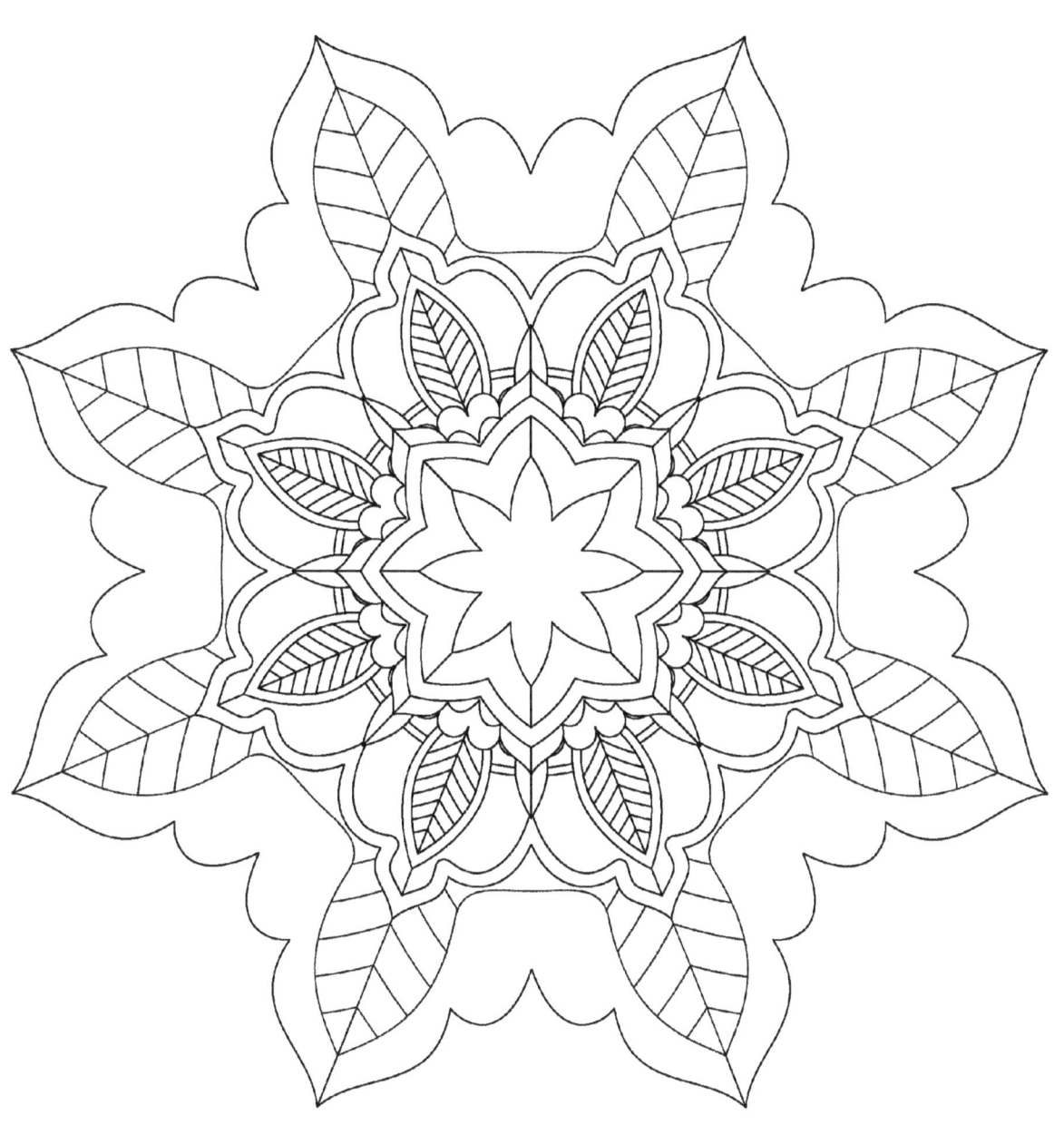

COLORS
TEST

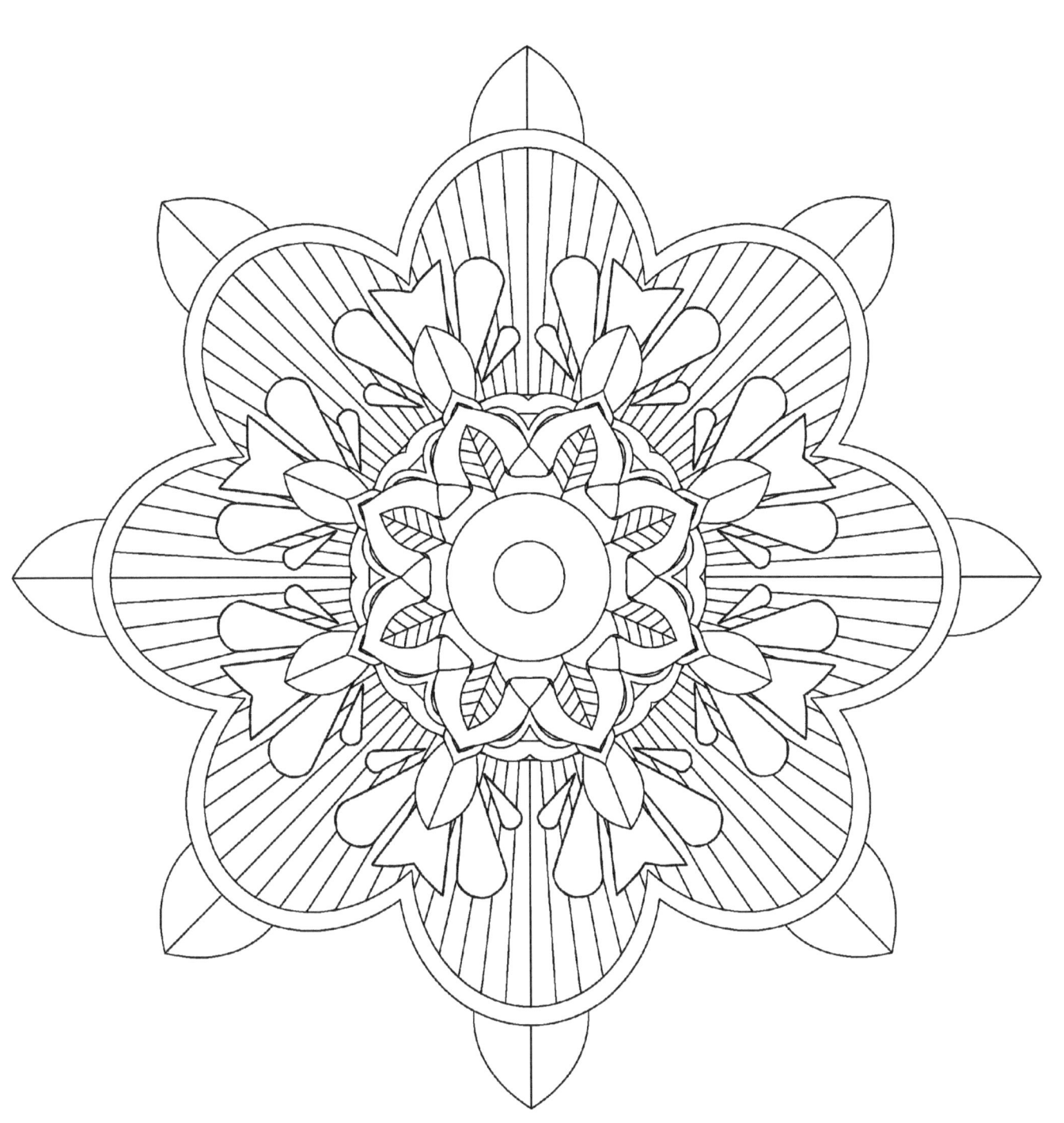

COLORS
TEST

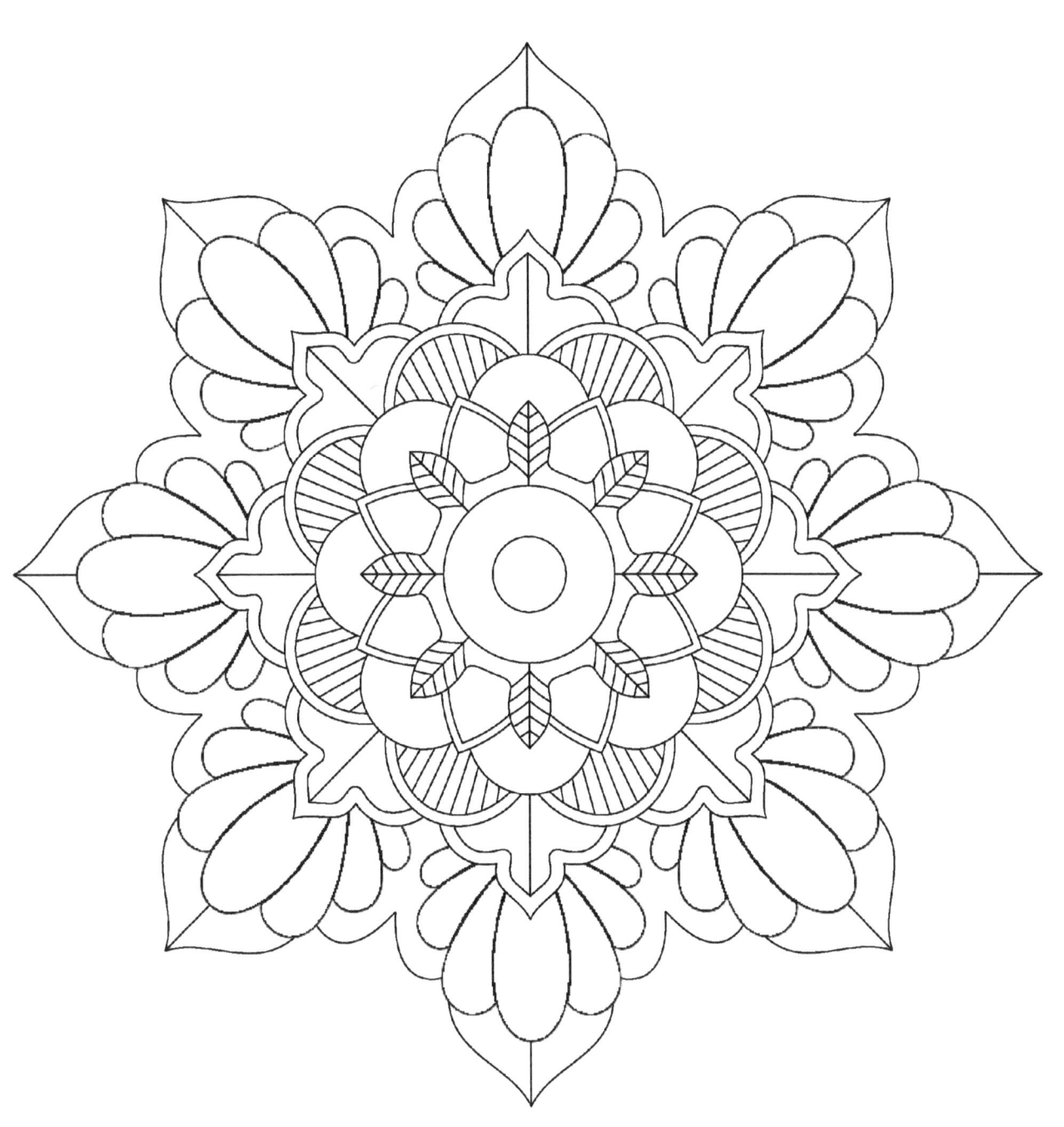

COLORS TEST

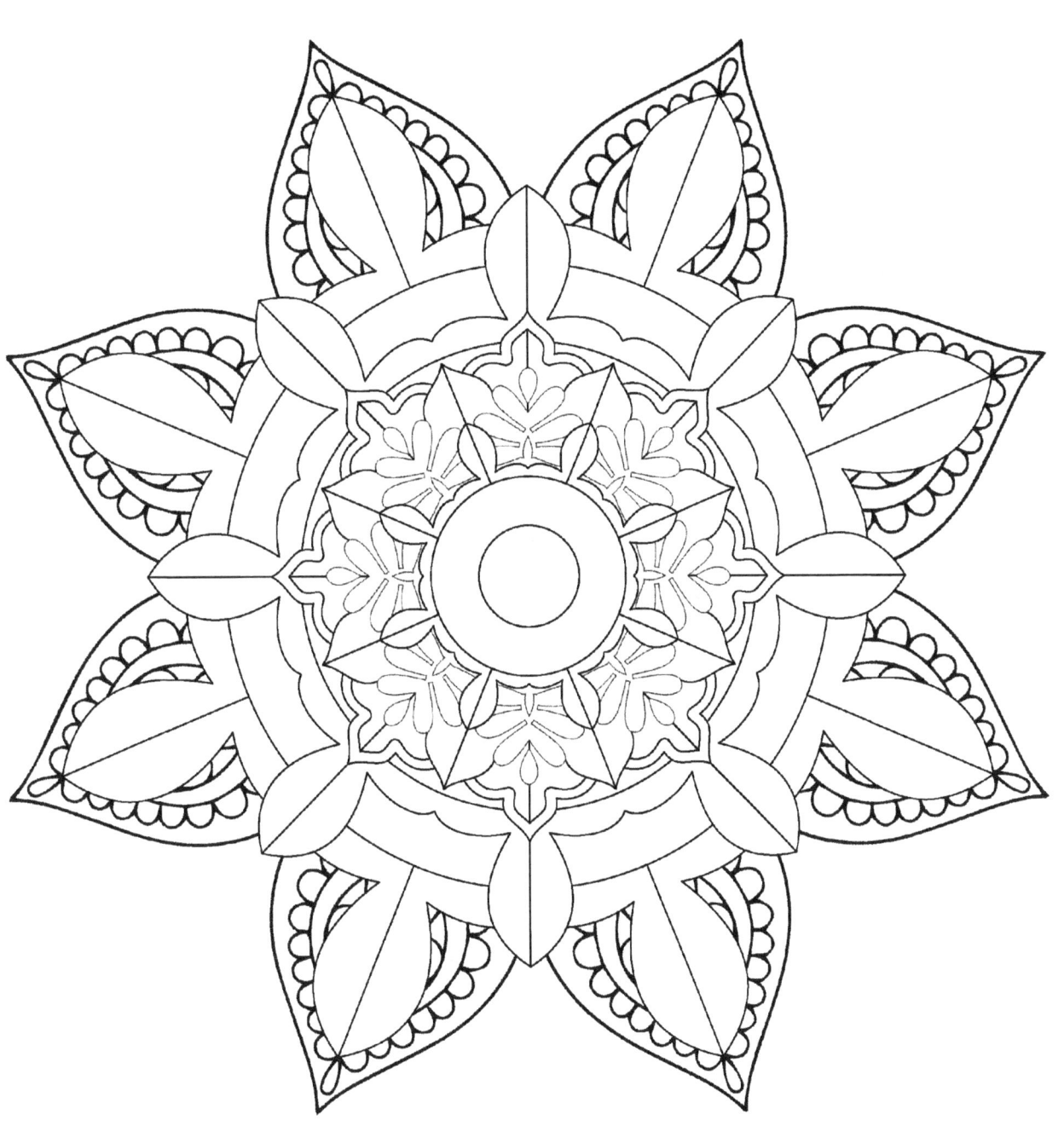

COLORS
TEST

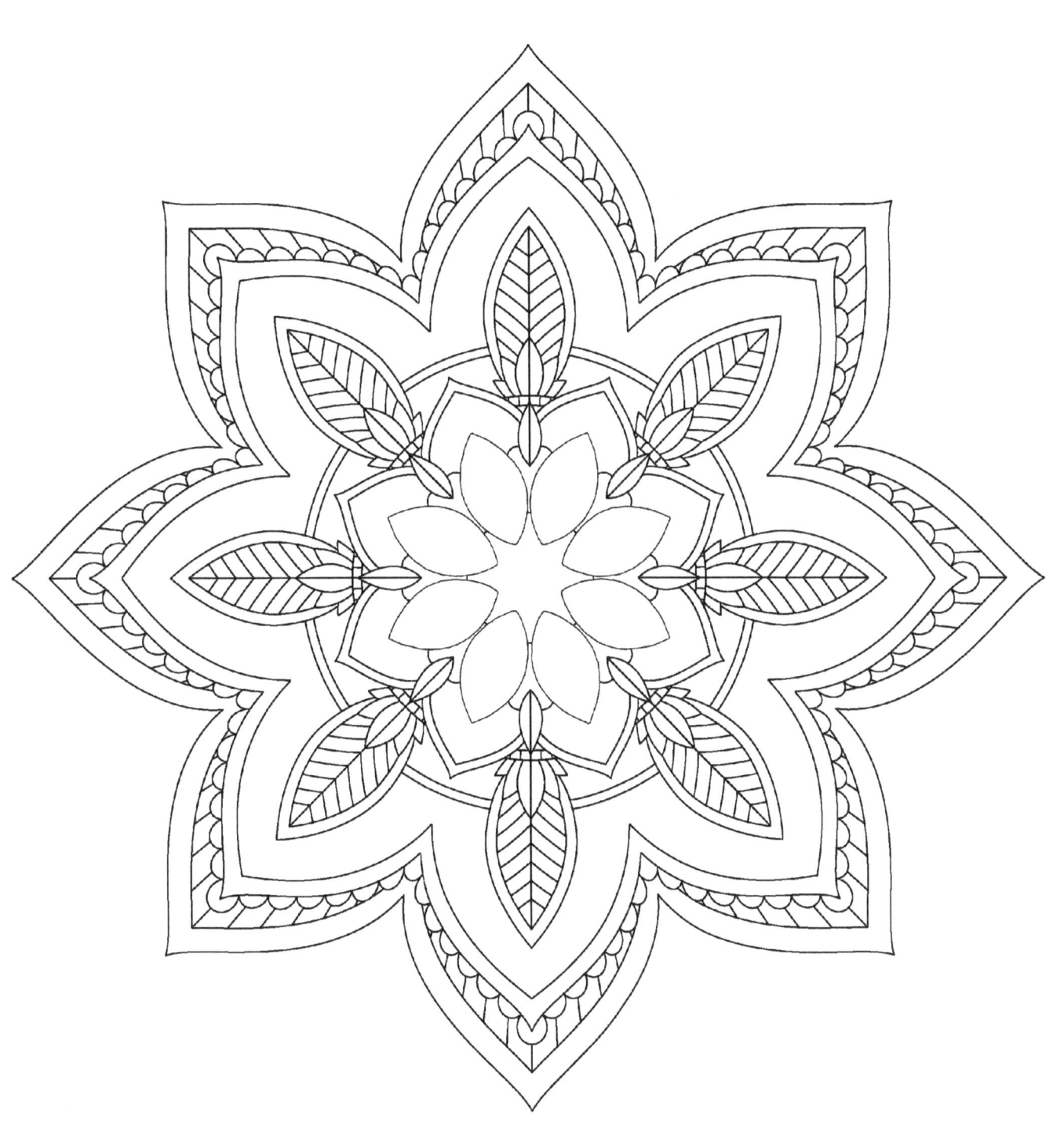

COLORS
TEST

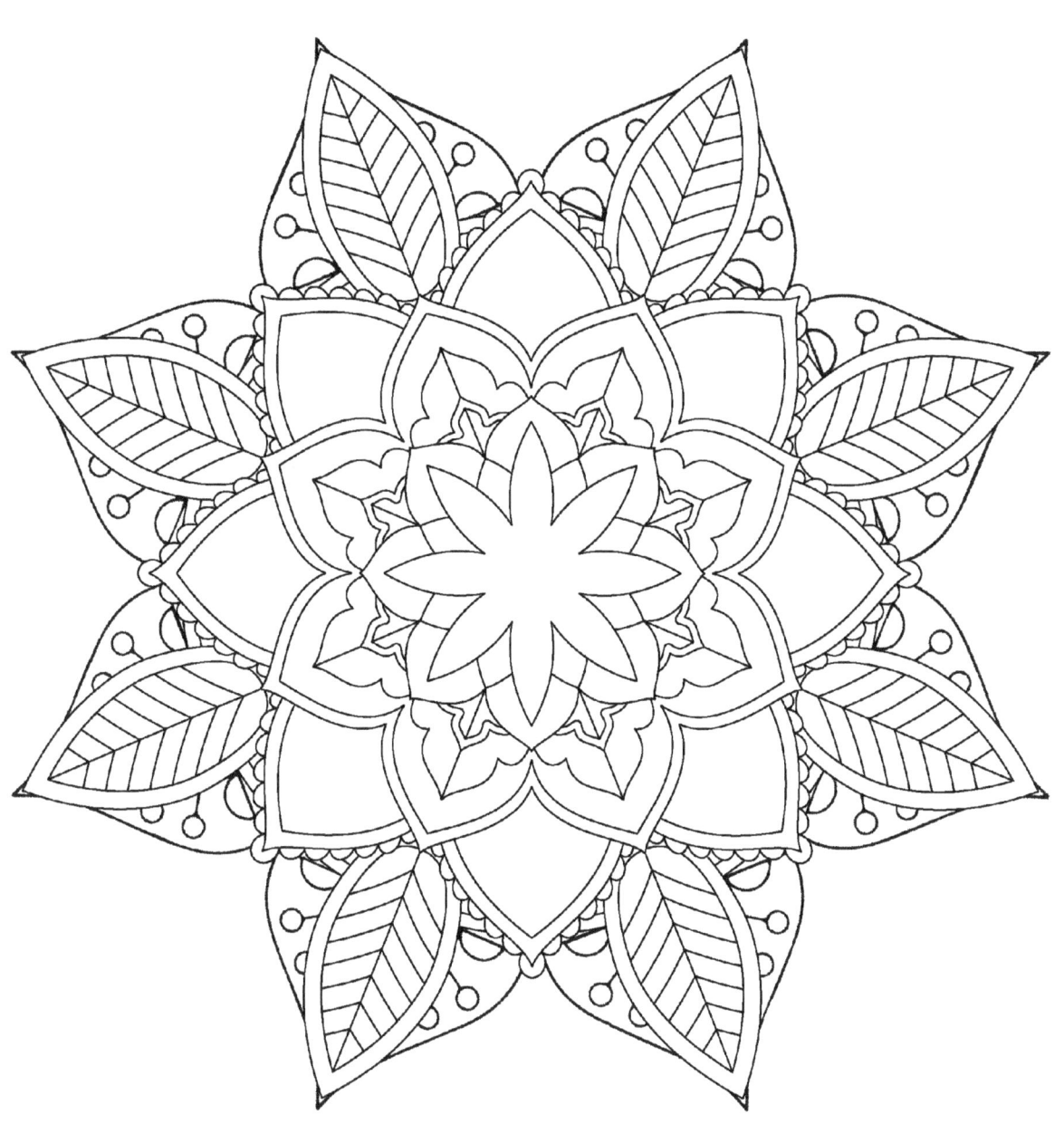

COLORS
TEST

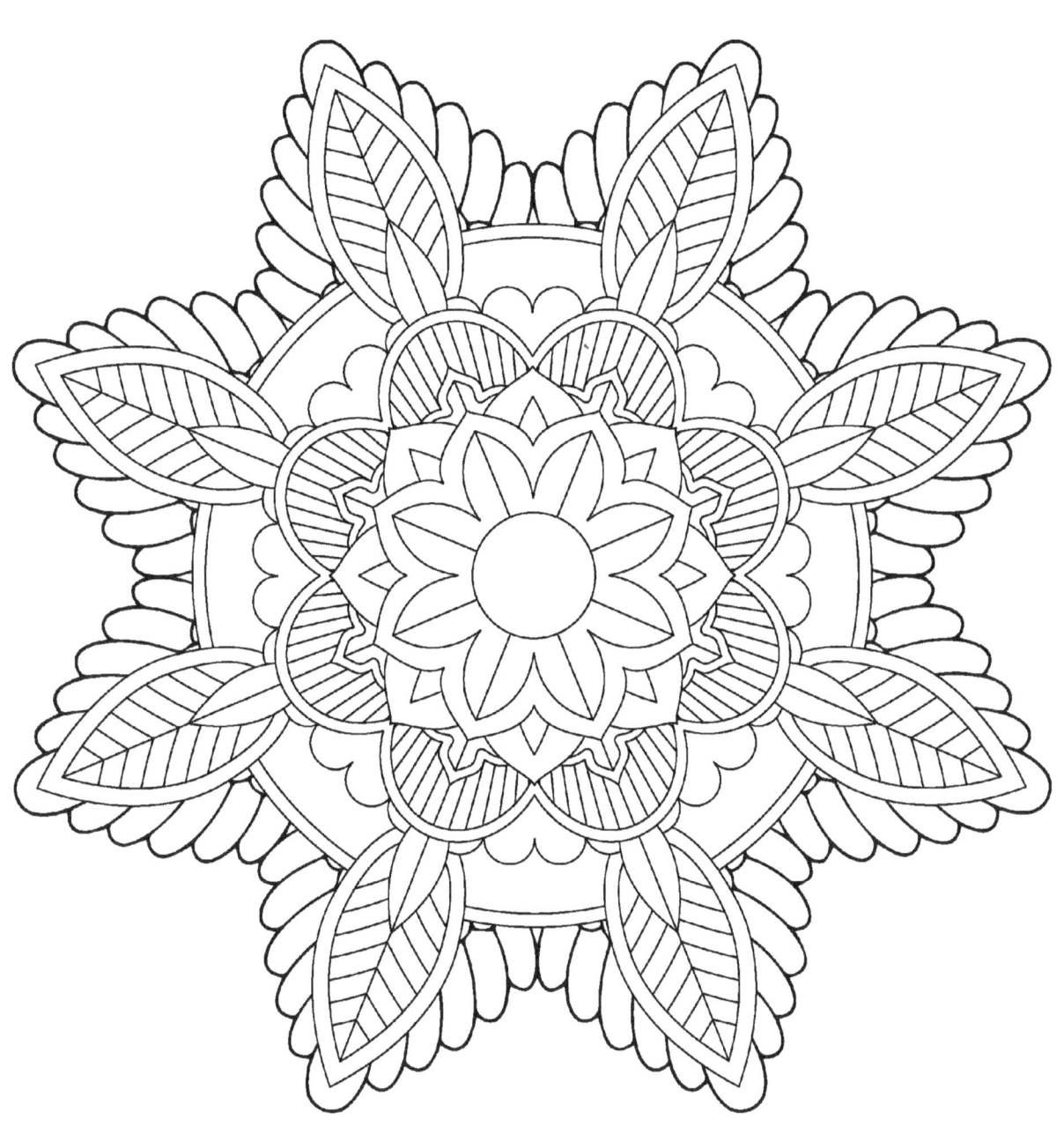

COLORS TEST

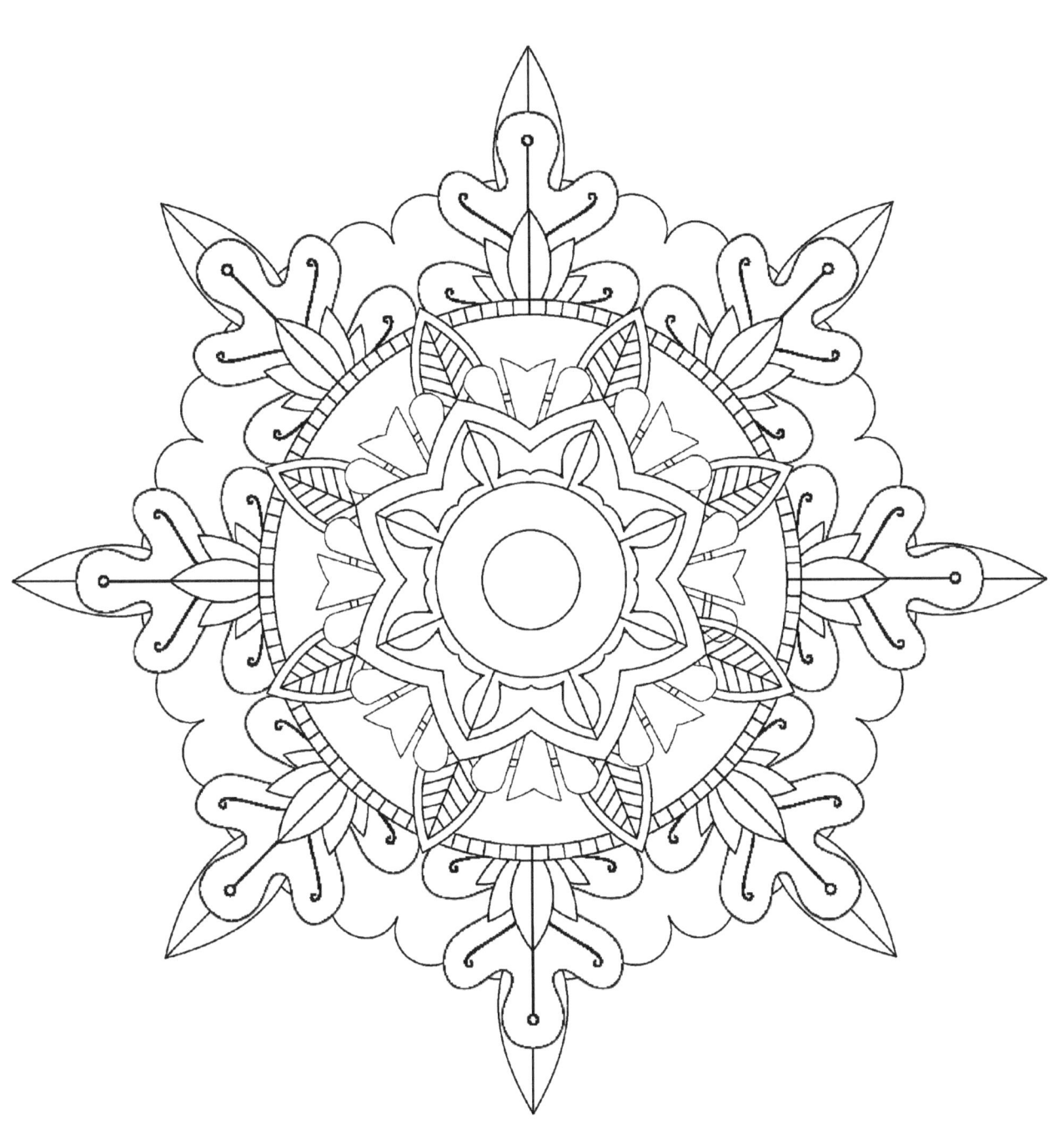

COLORS
TEST

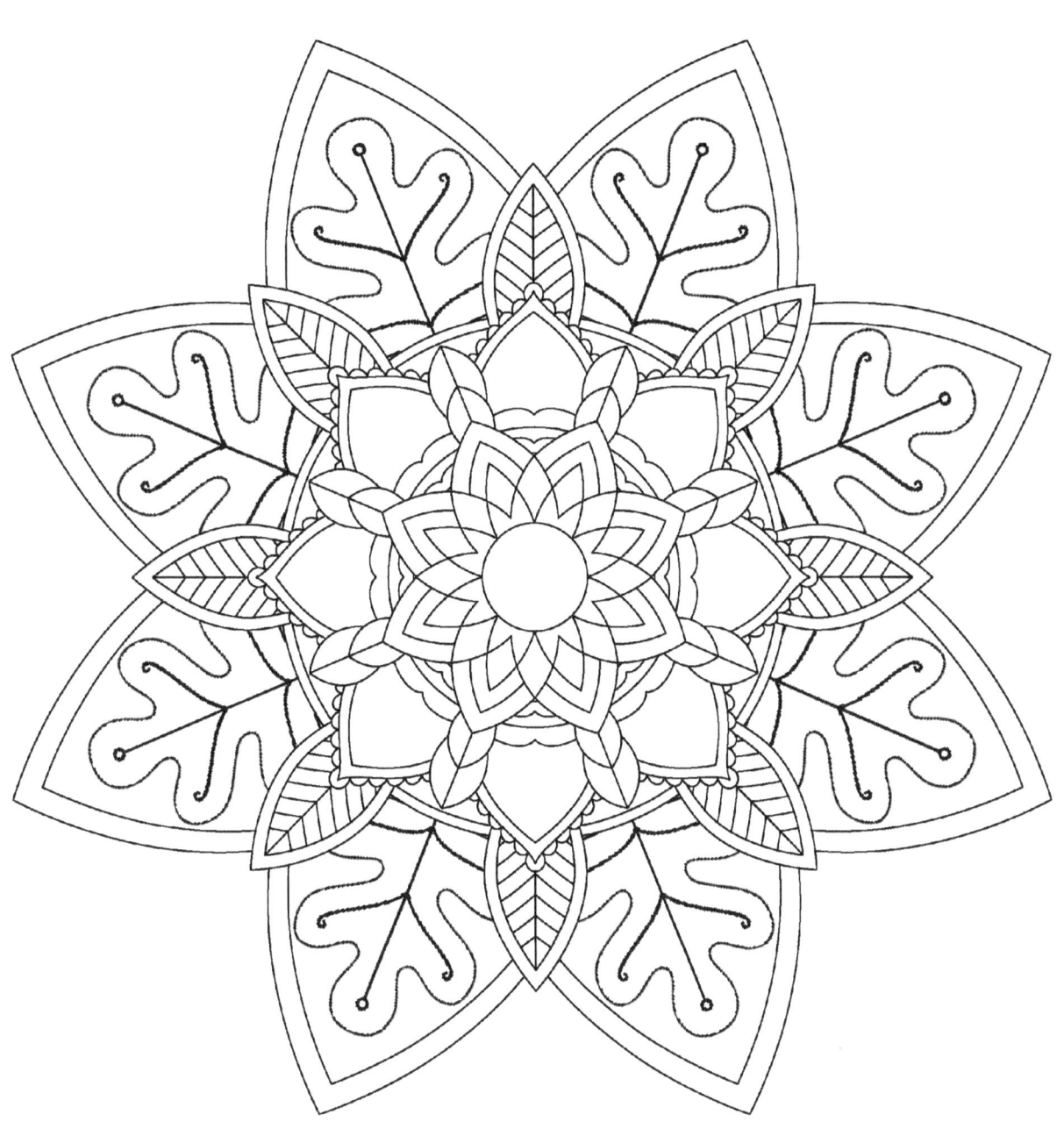

COLORS
TEST

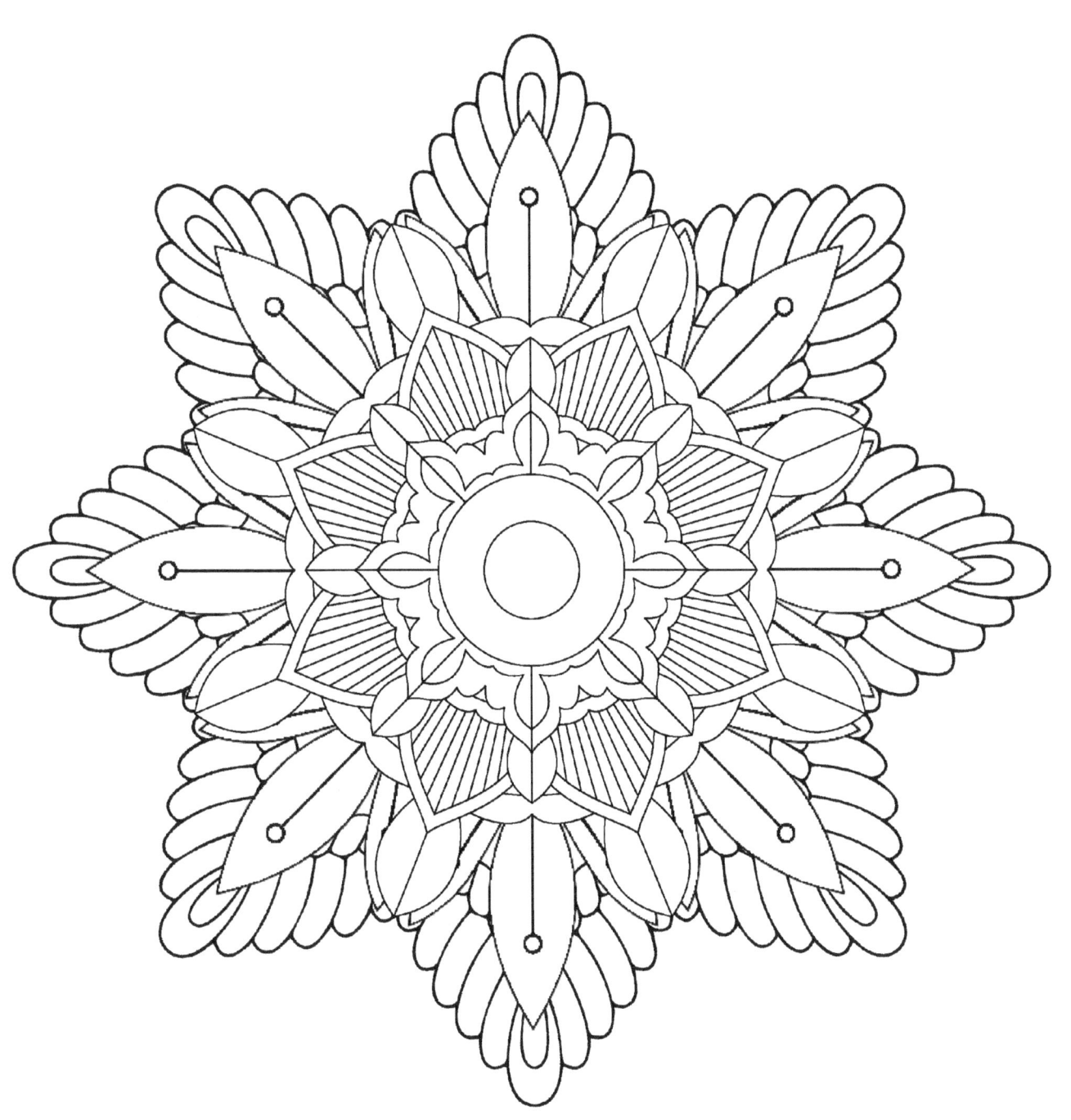

COLORS
TEST

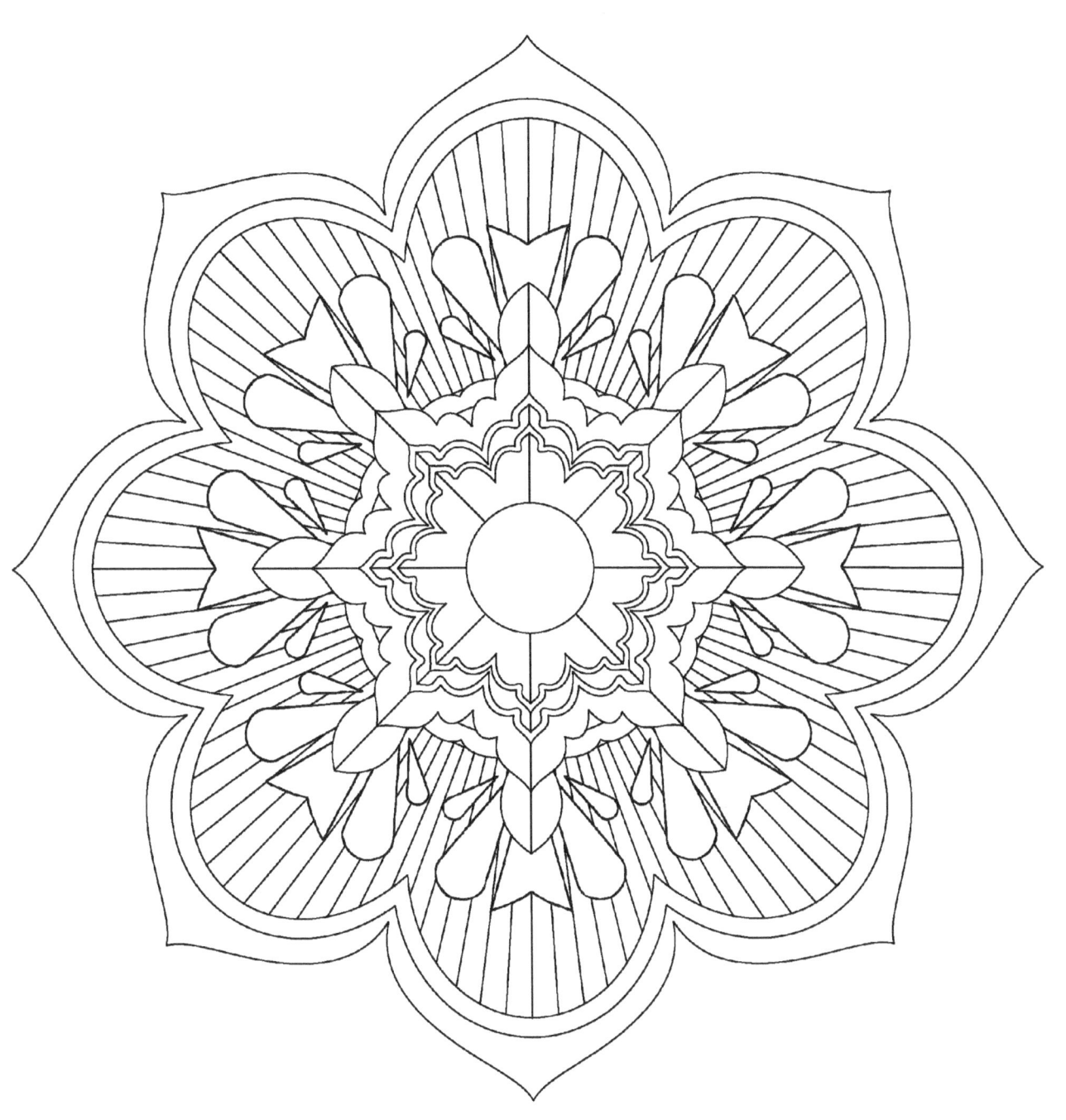

COLORS
TEST

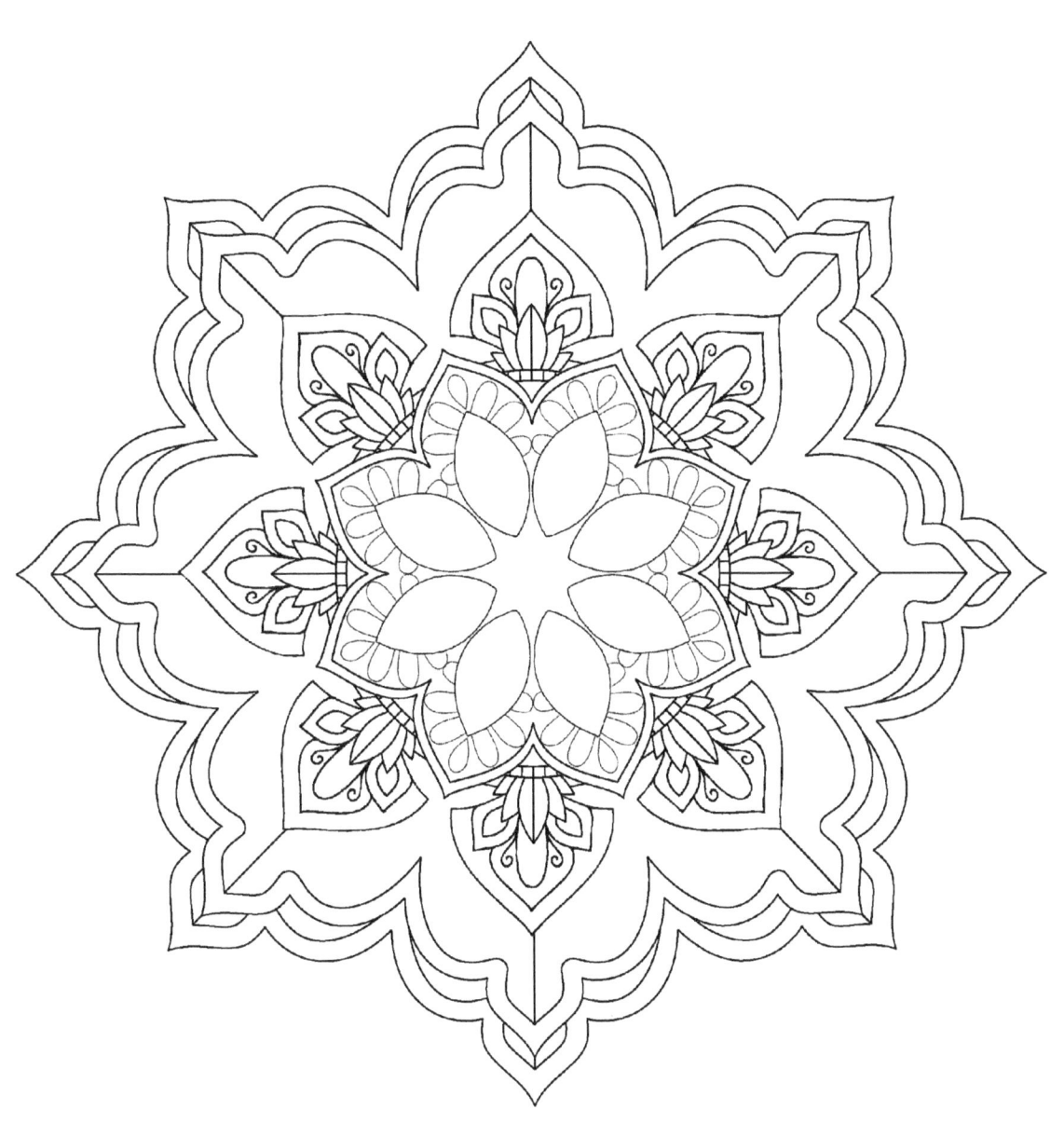

COLORS
TEST

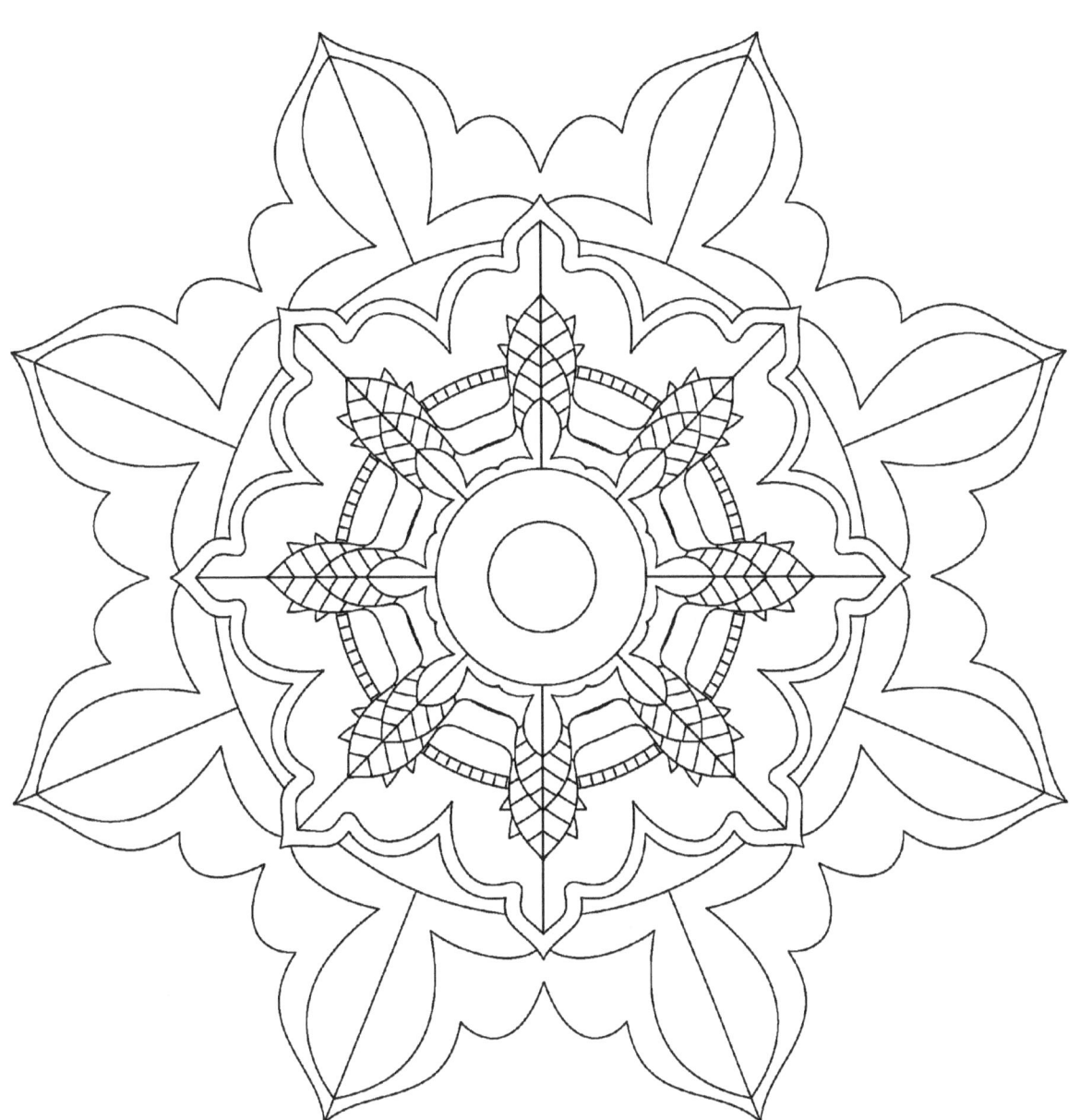

COLORS
TEST

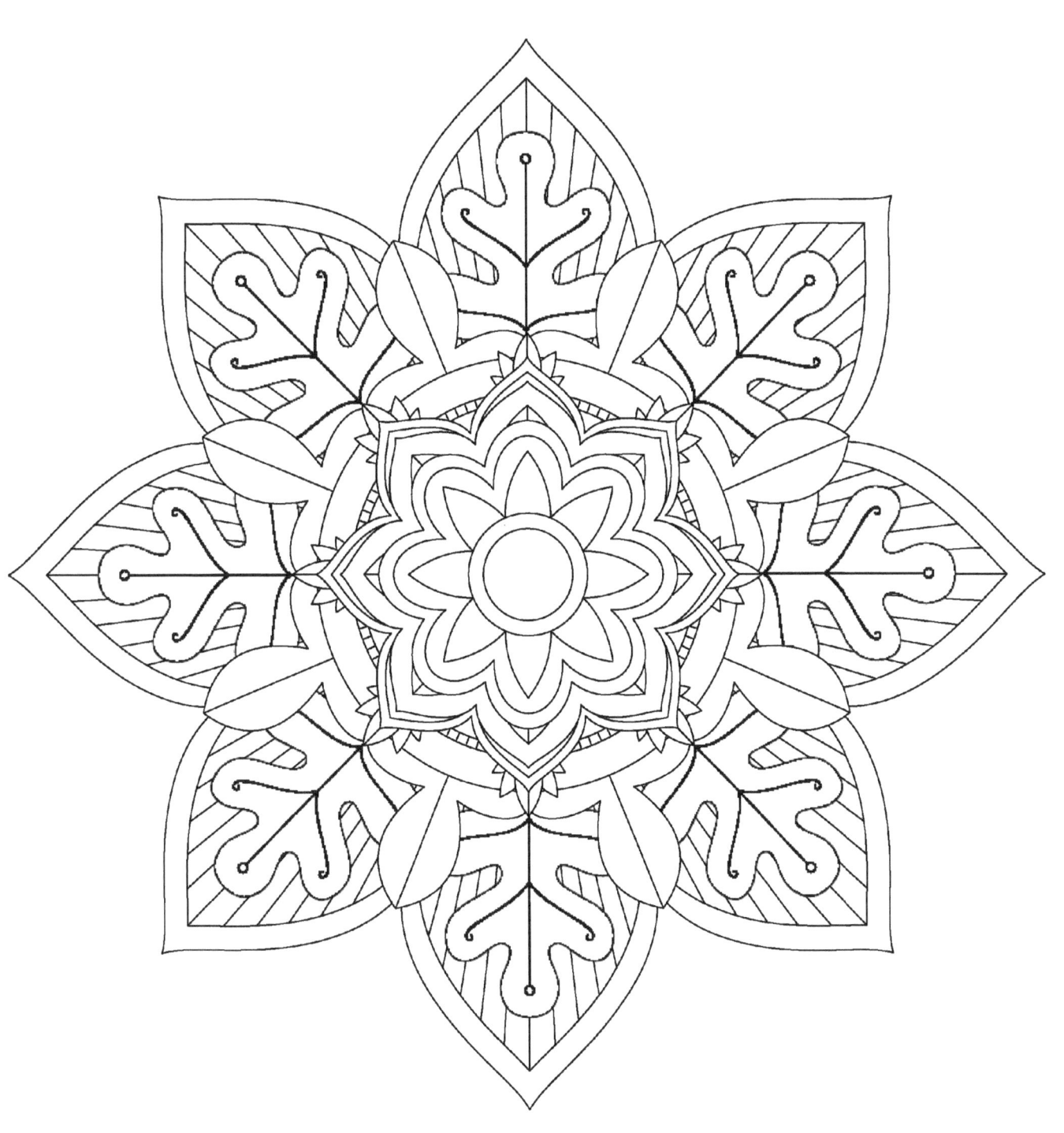

COLORS
TEST

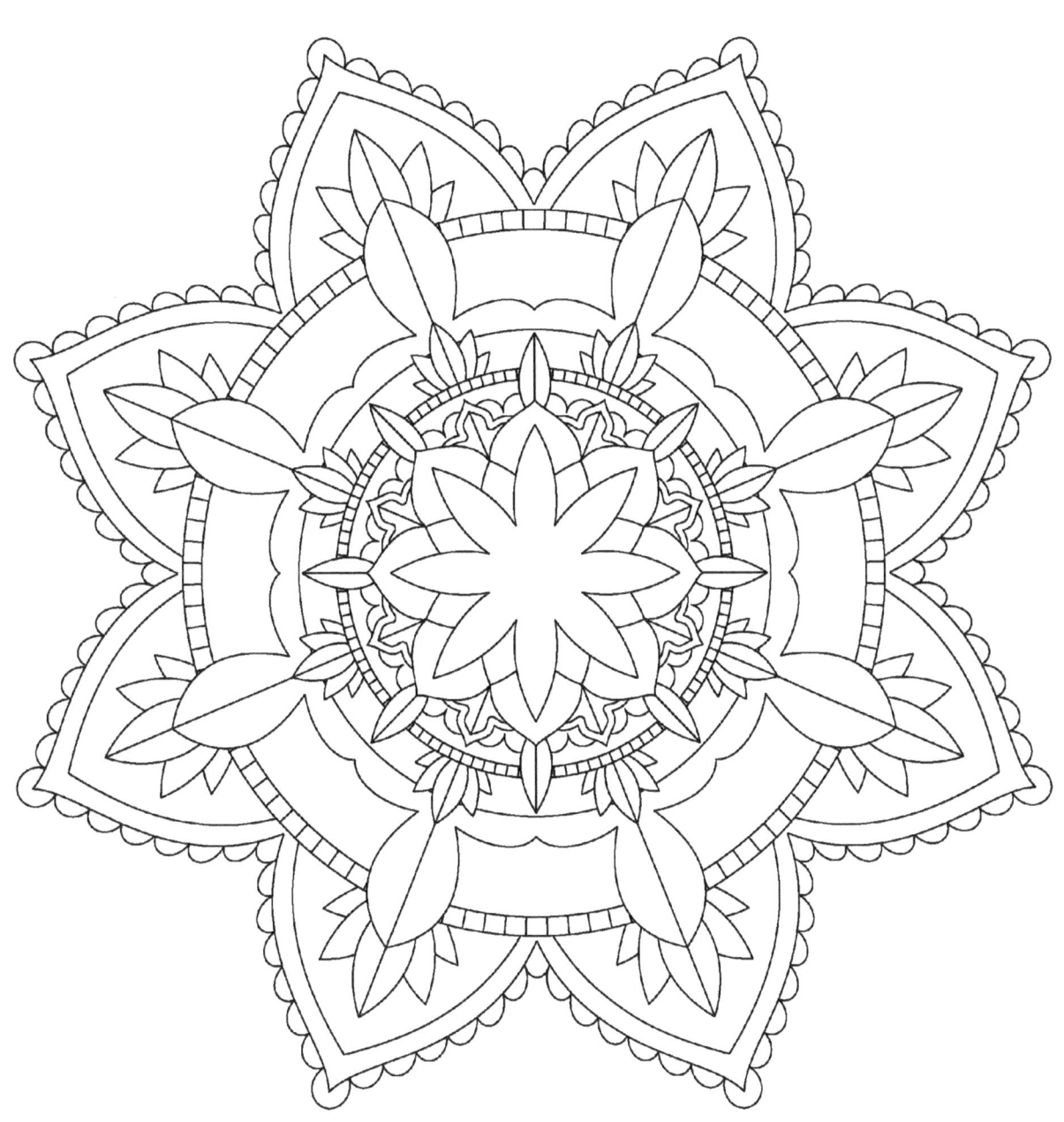

COLORS TEST

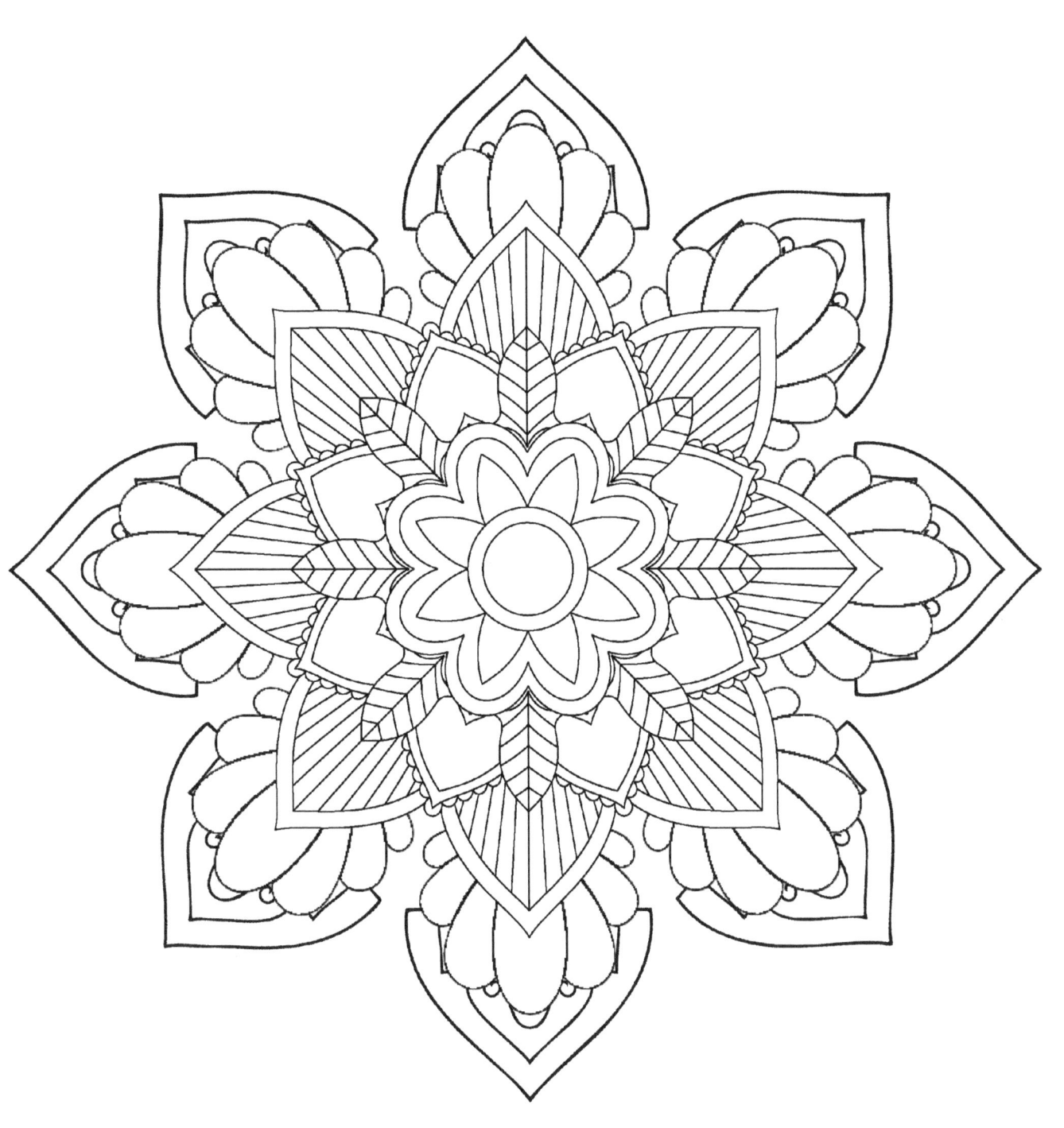

COLORS TEST

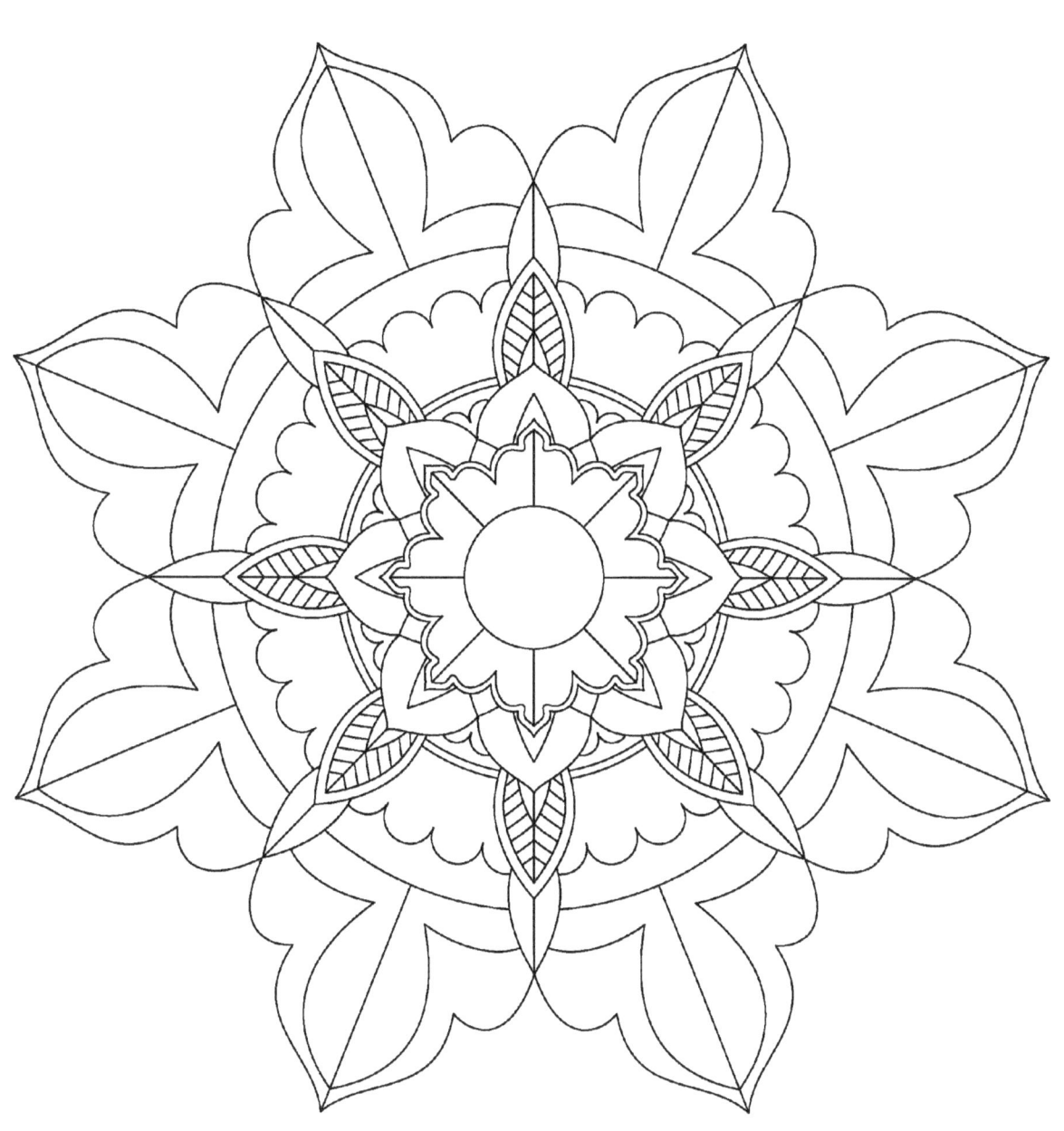

COLORS
TEST

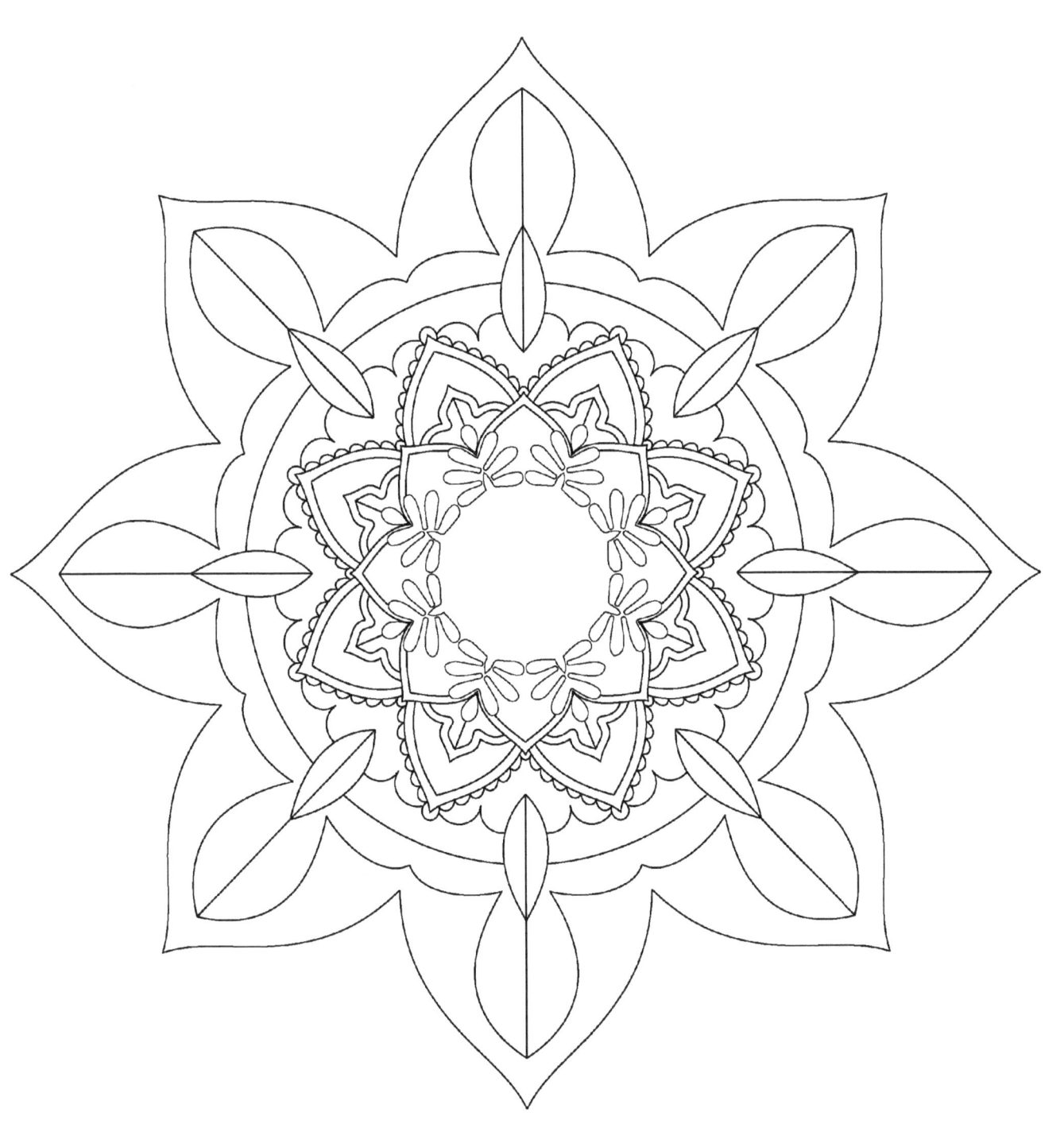

COLORS
TEST

COLORS
TEST

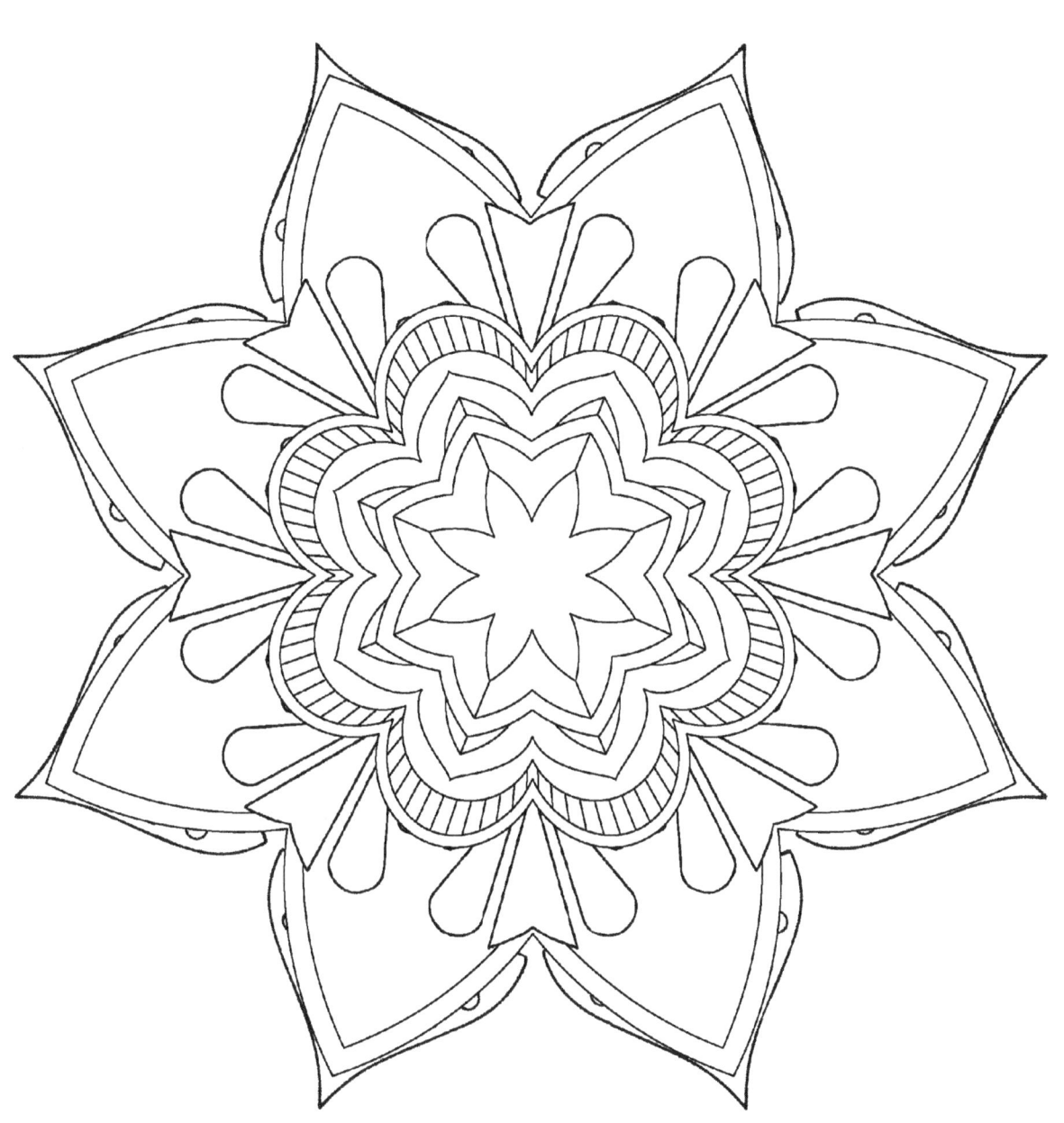

COLORS
TEST

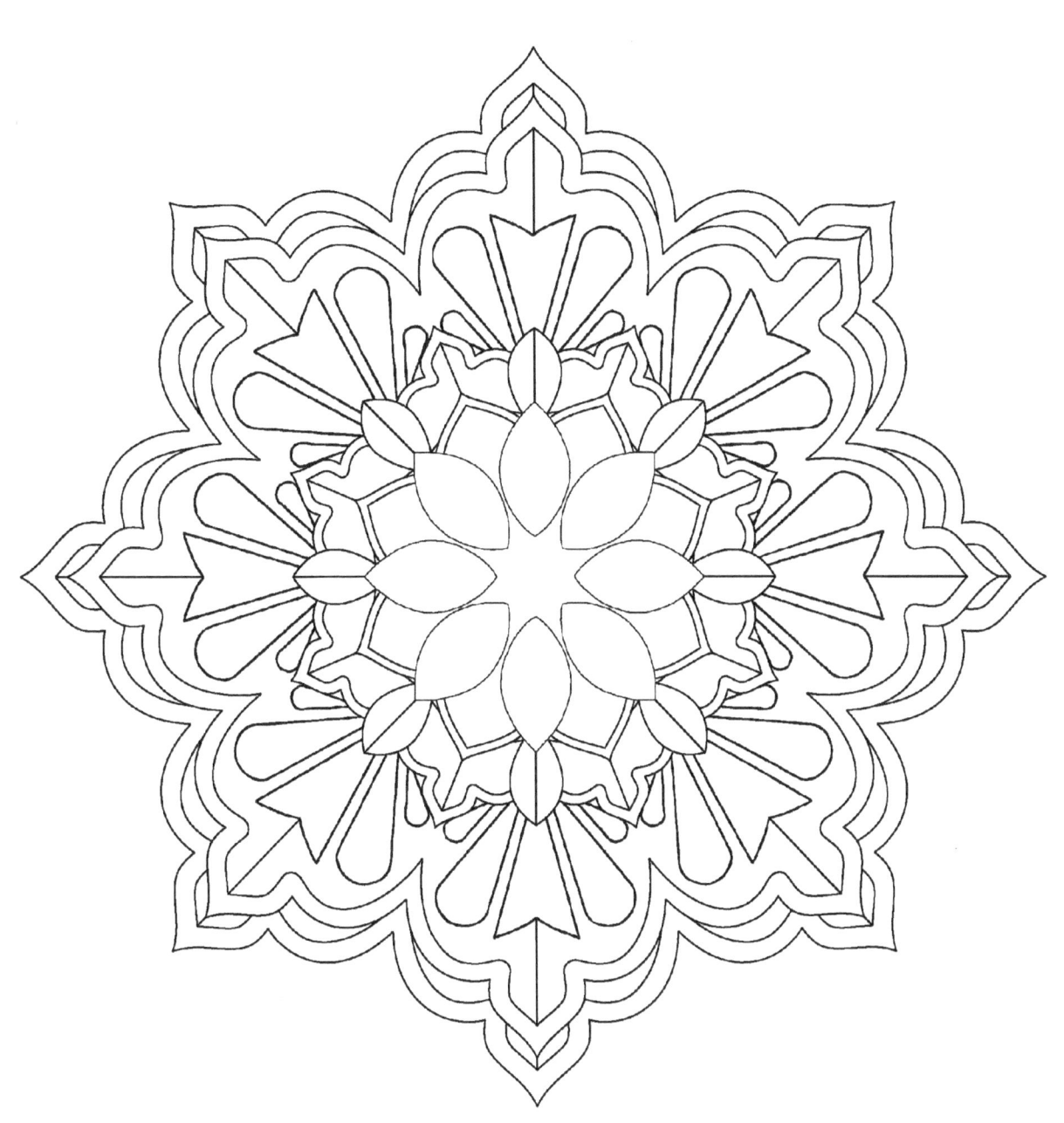

COLORS
TEST

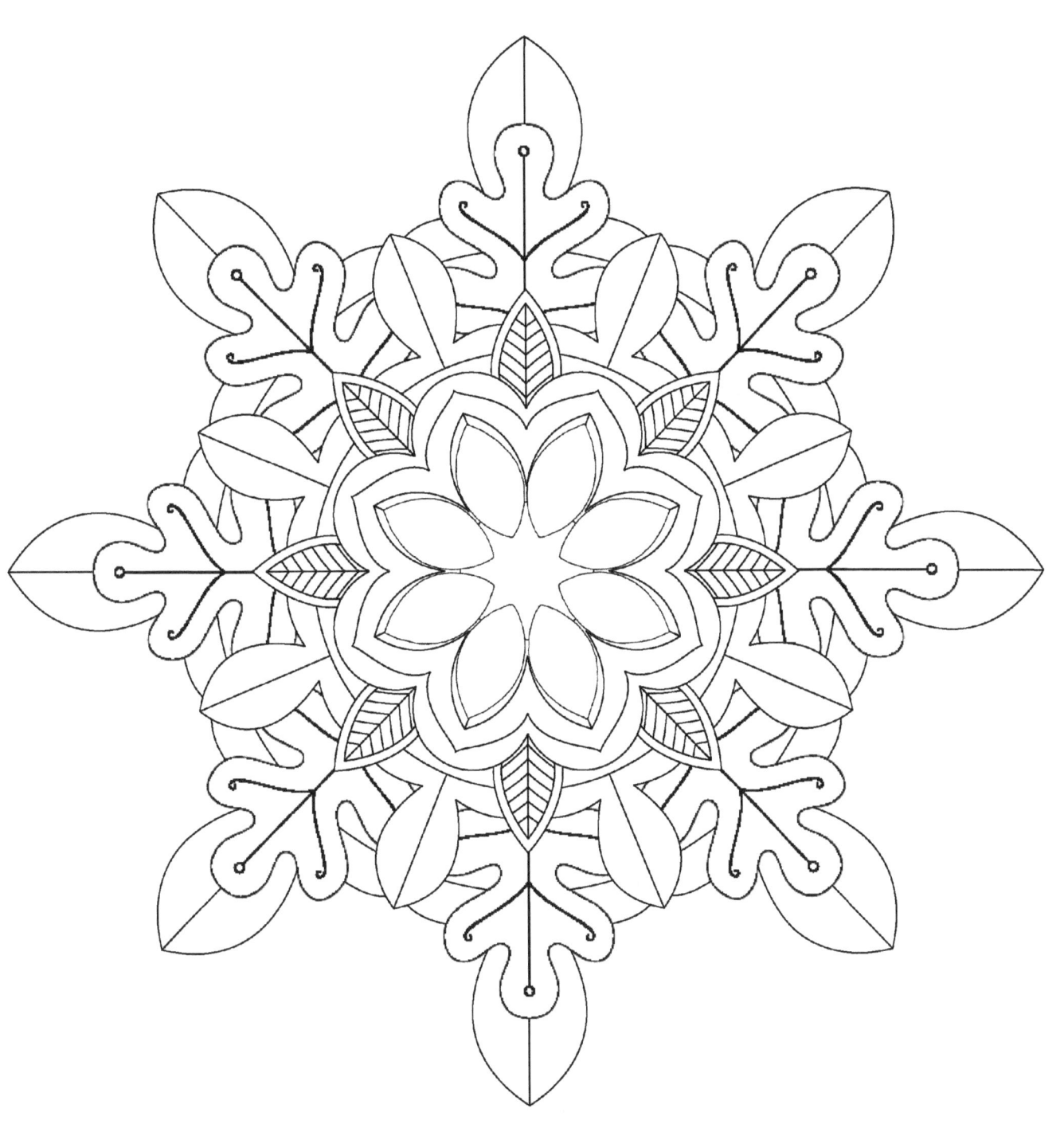

COLORS
TEST

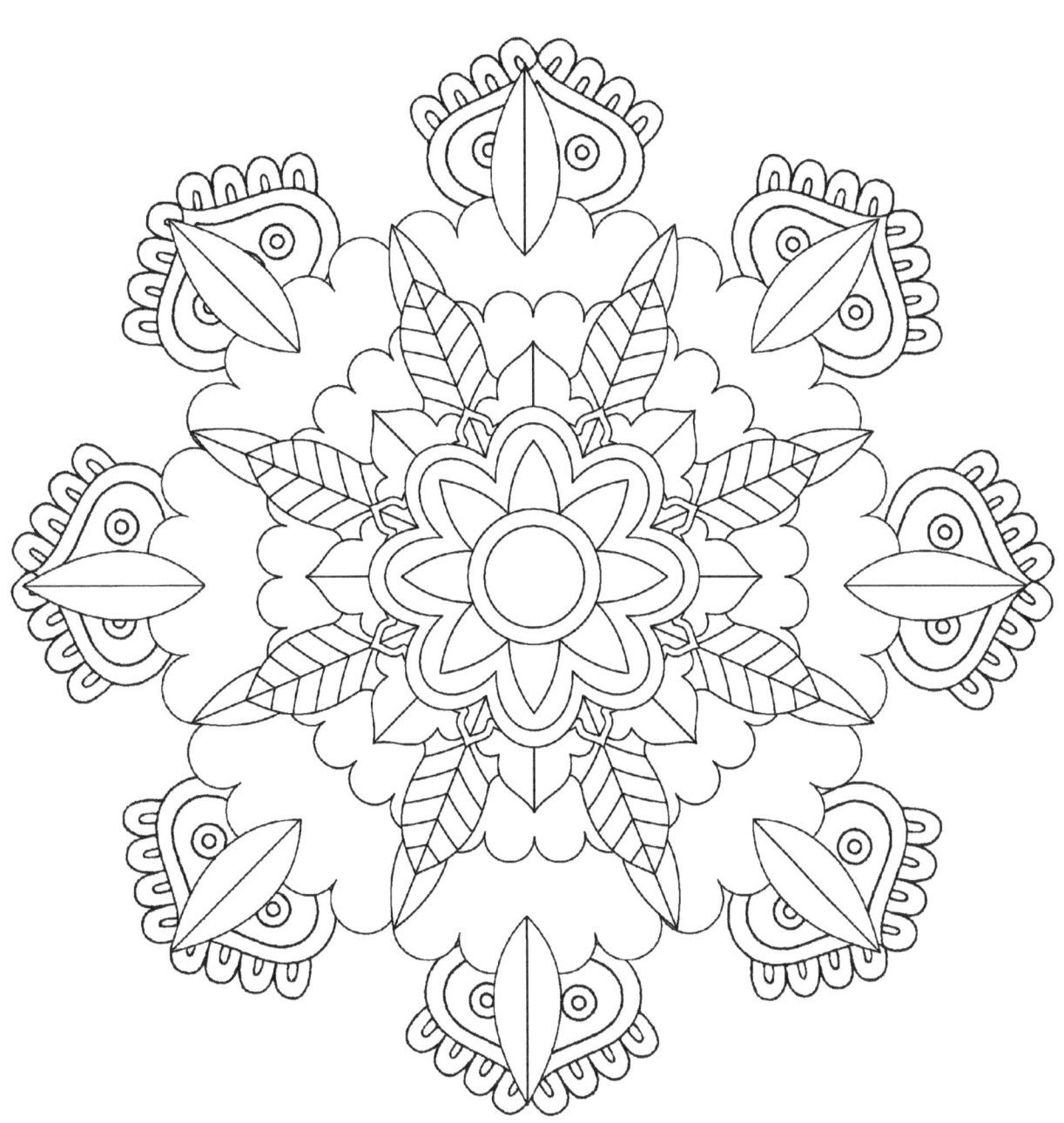

COLORS
TEST

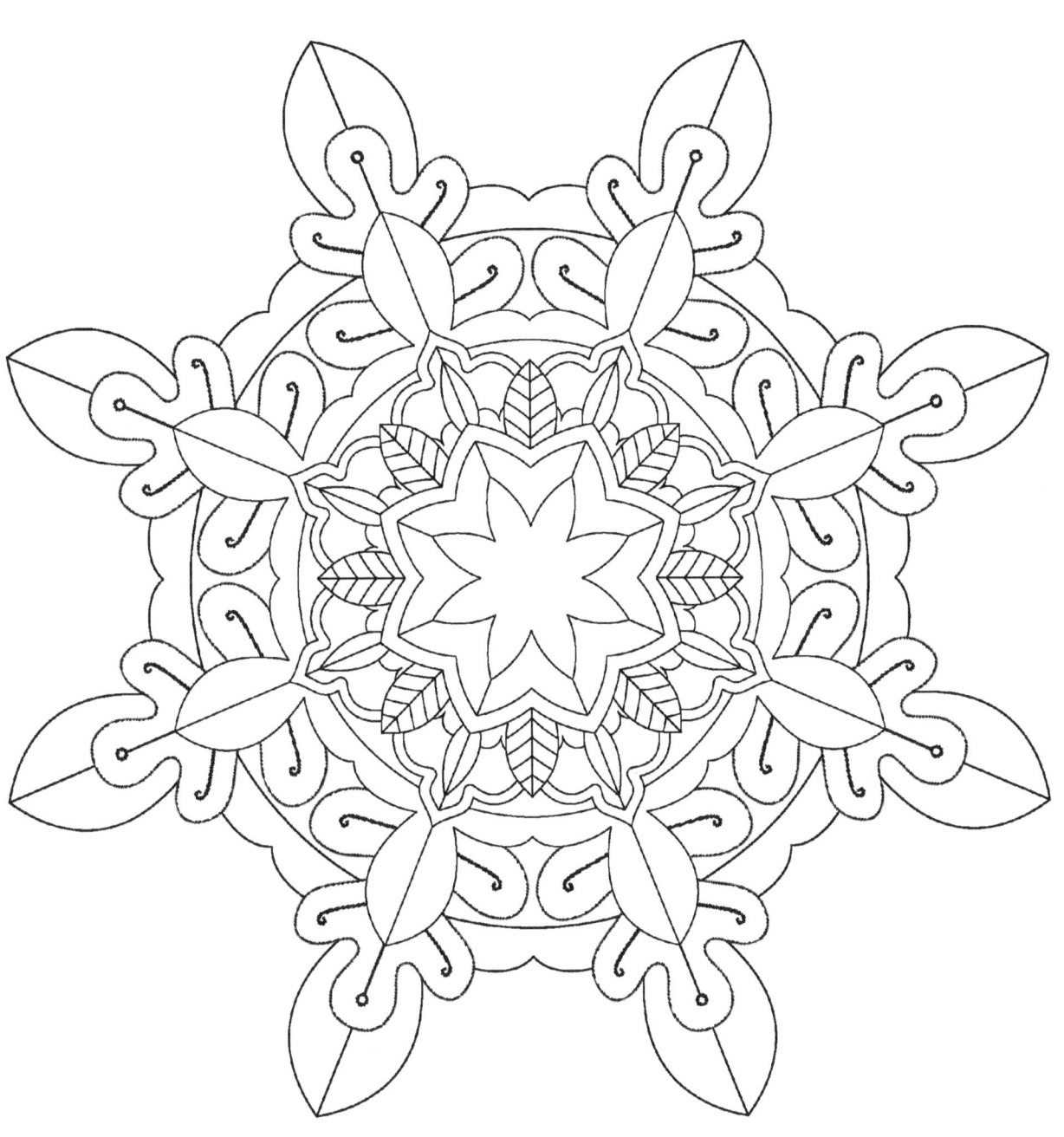

COLORS
TEST

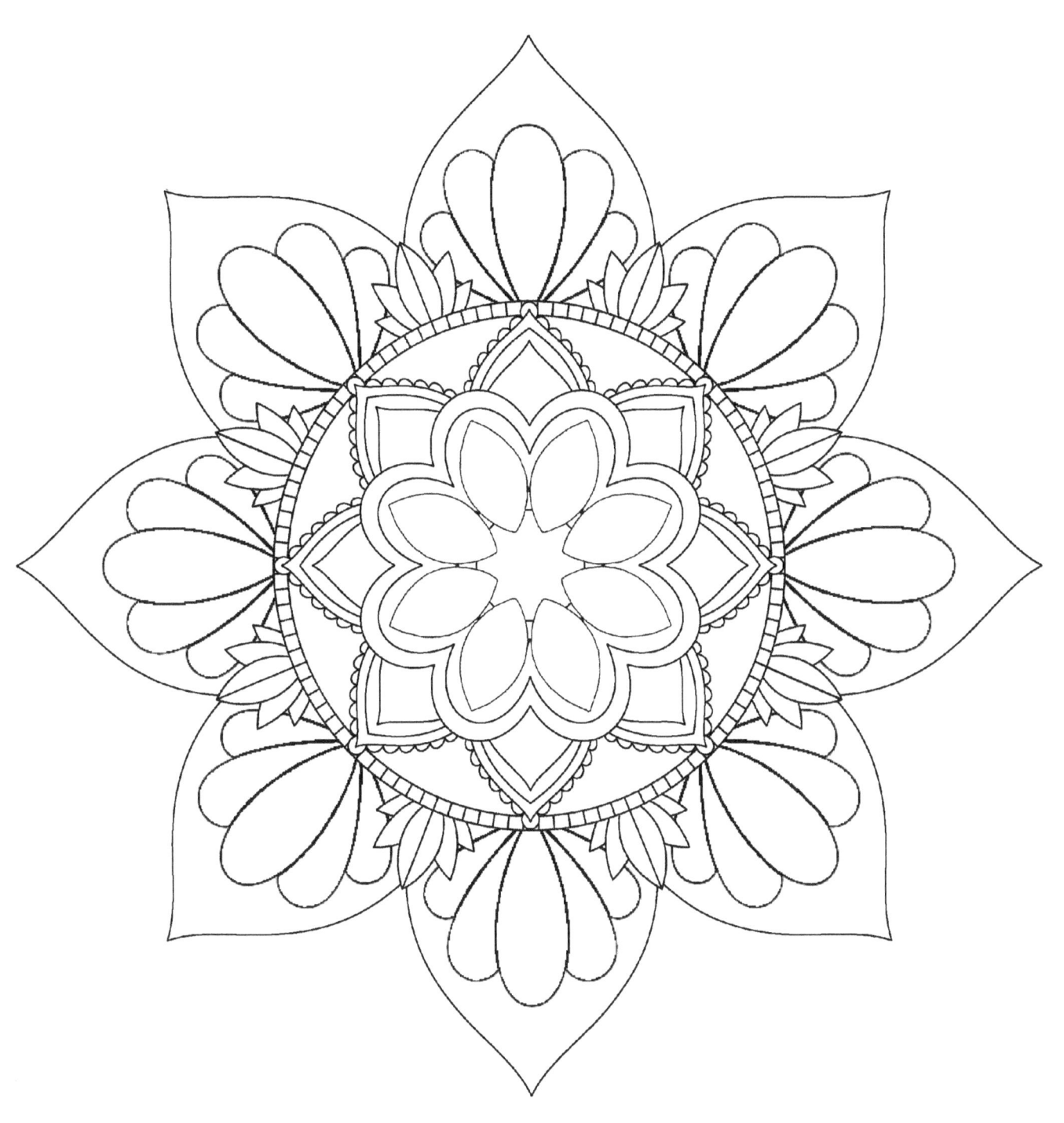

COLORS TEST

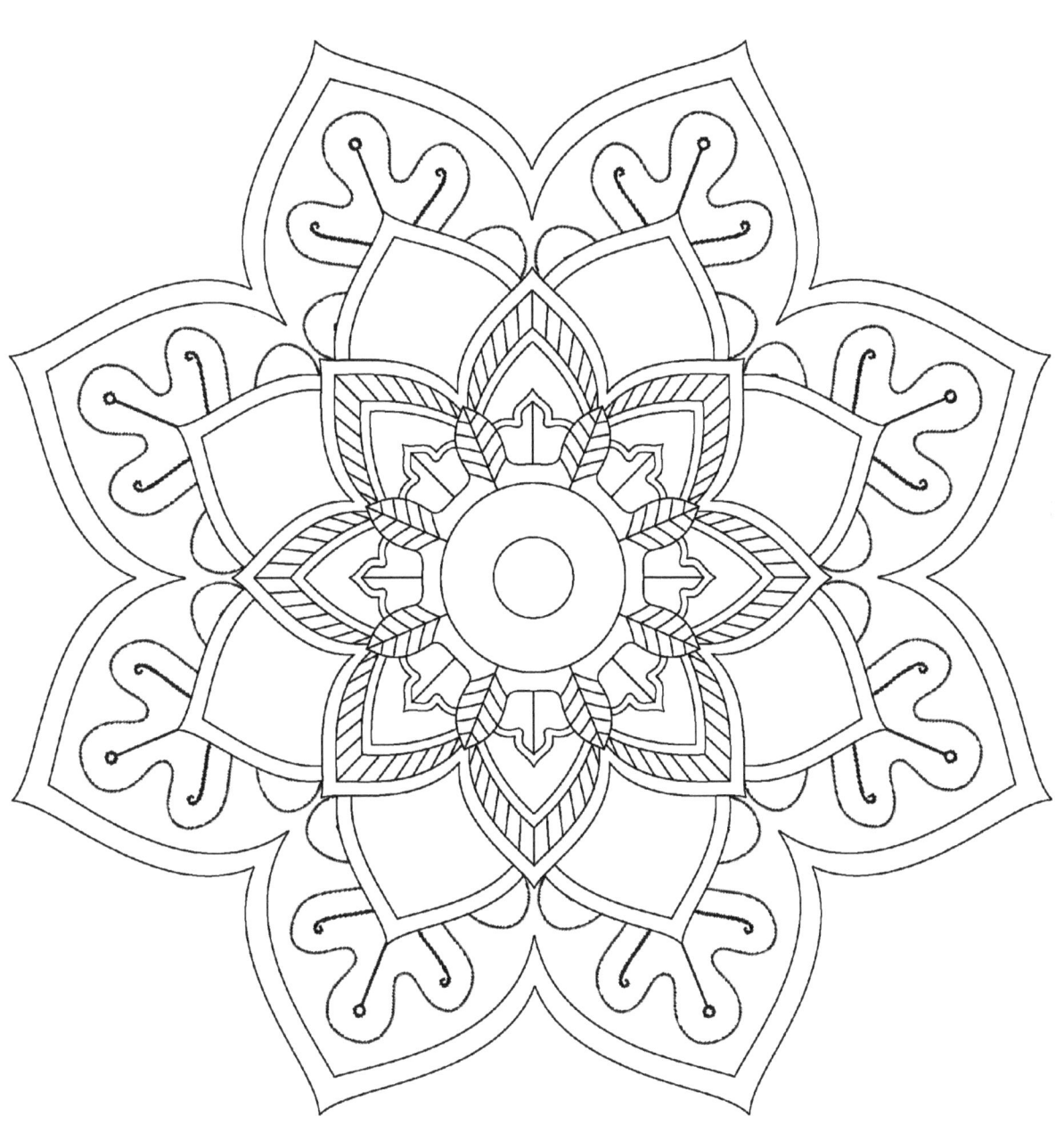

COLORS
TEST

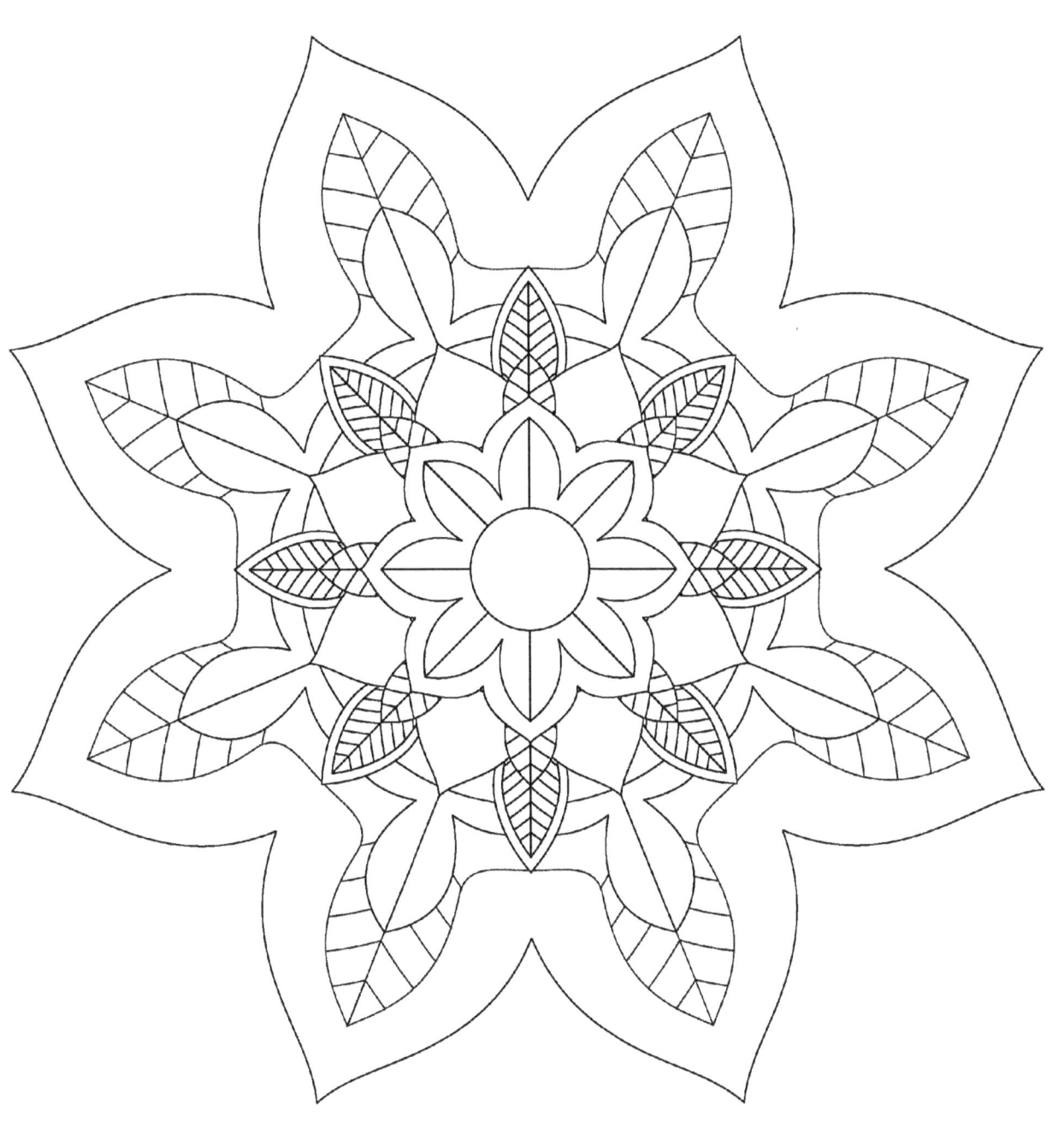

COLORS TEST

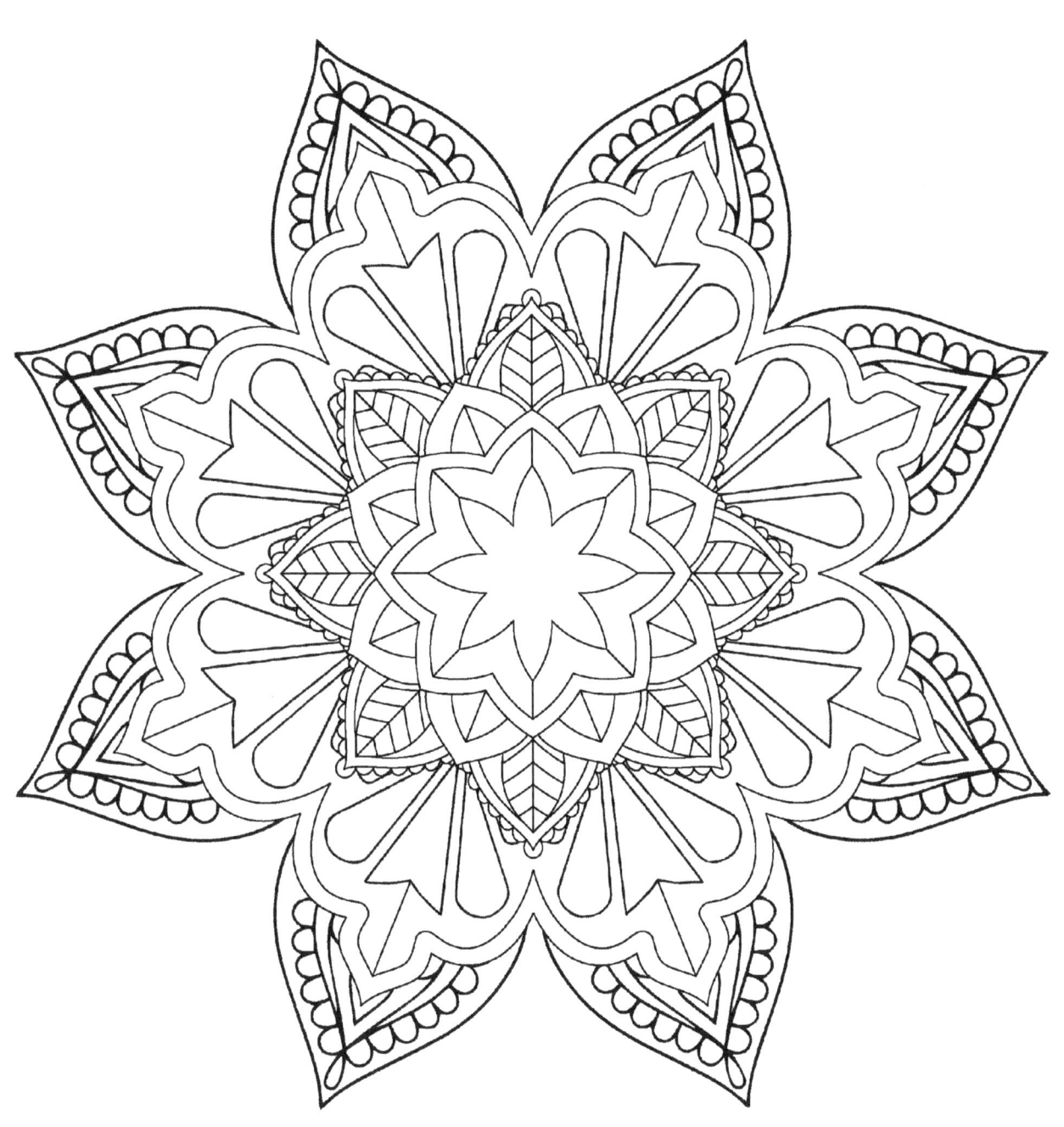

COLORS TEST

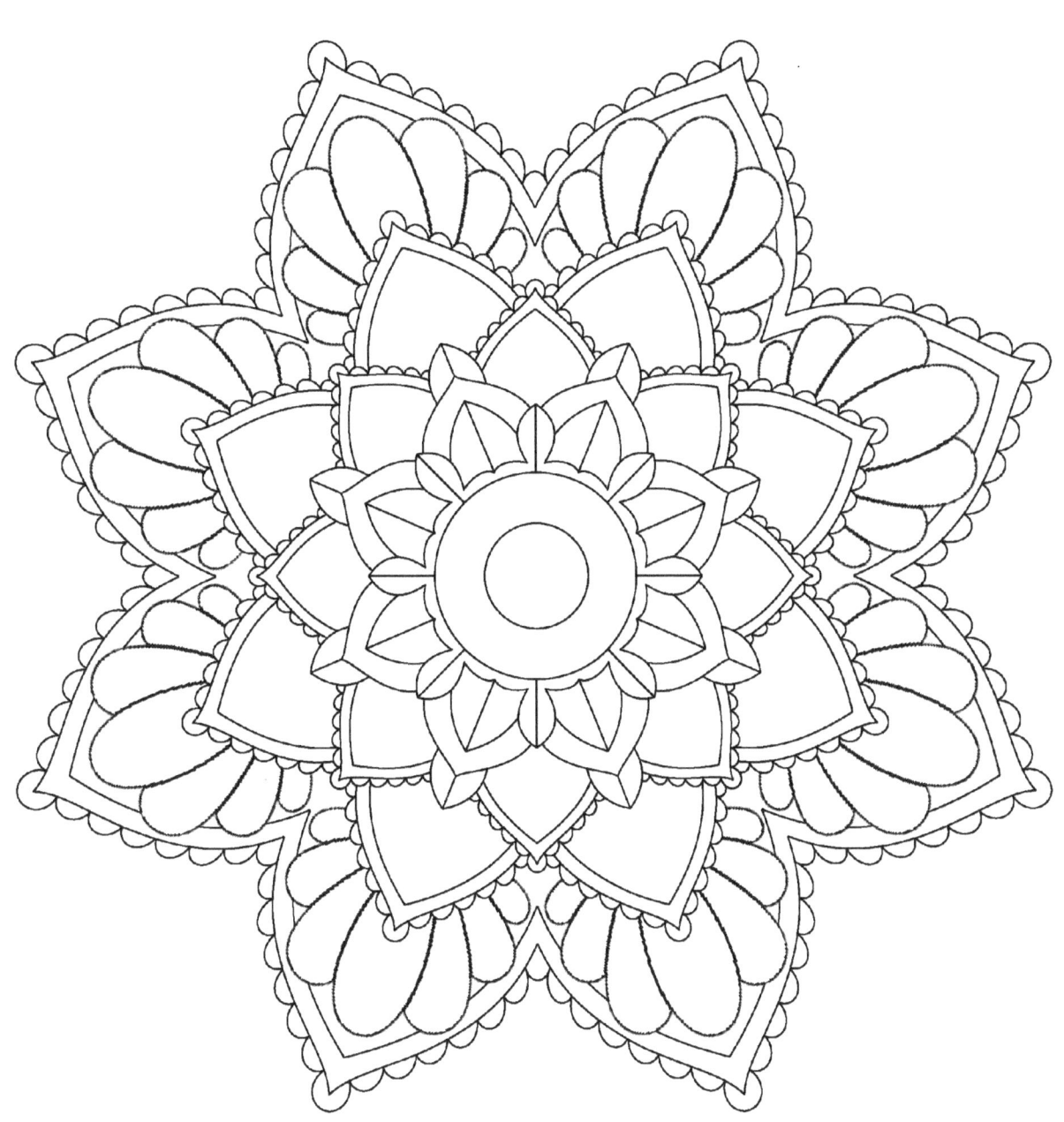

COLORS
TEST

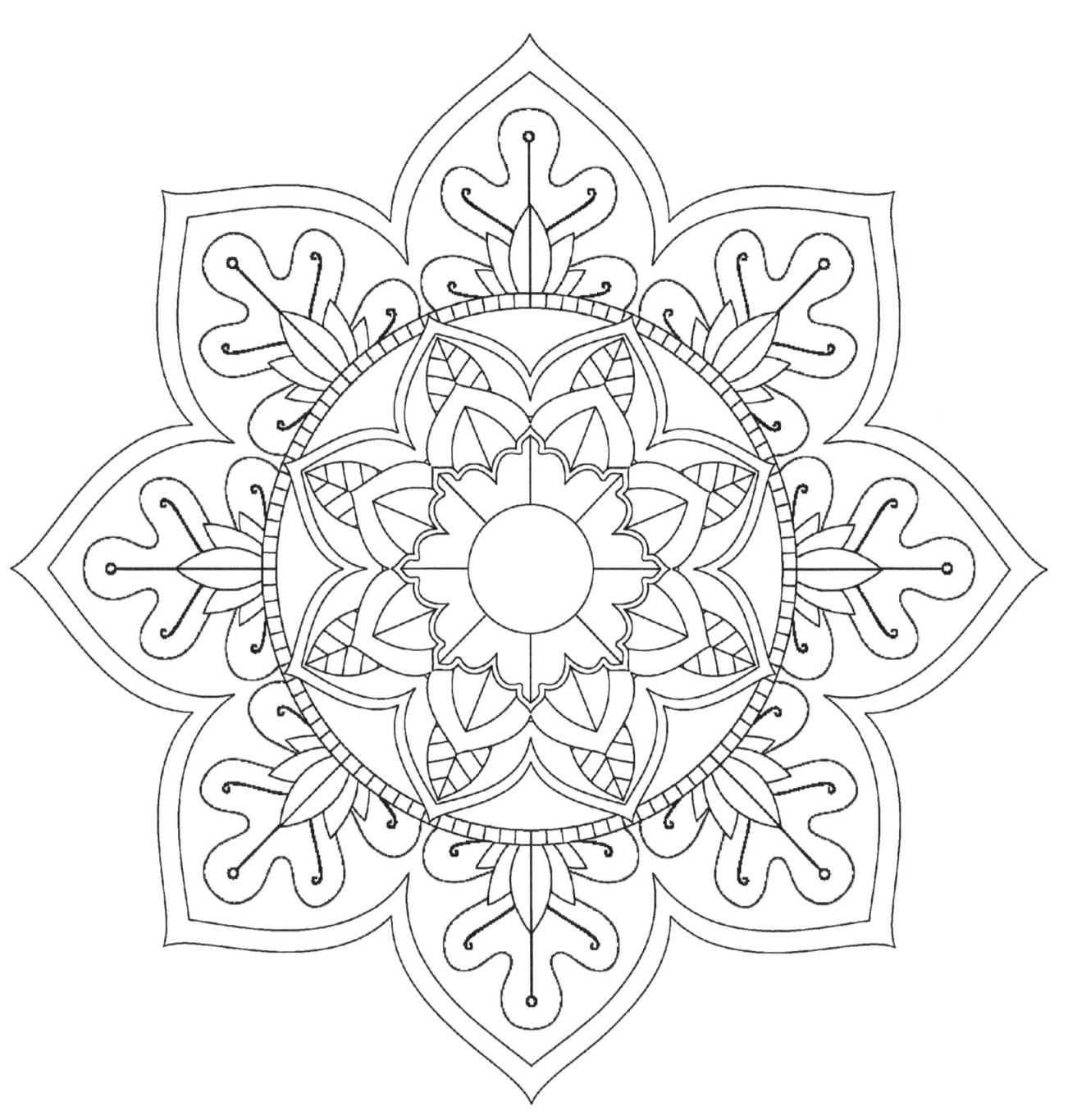

COLORS
TEST

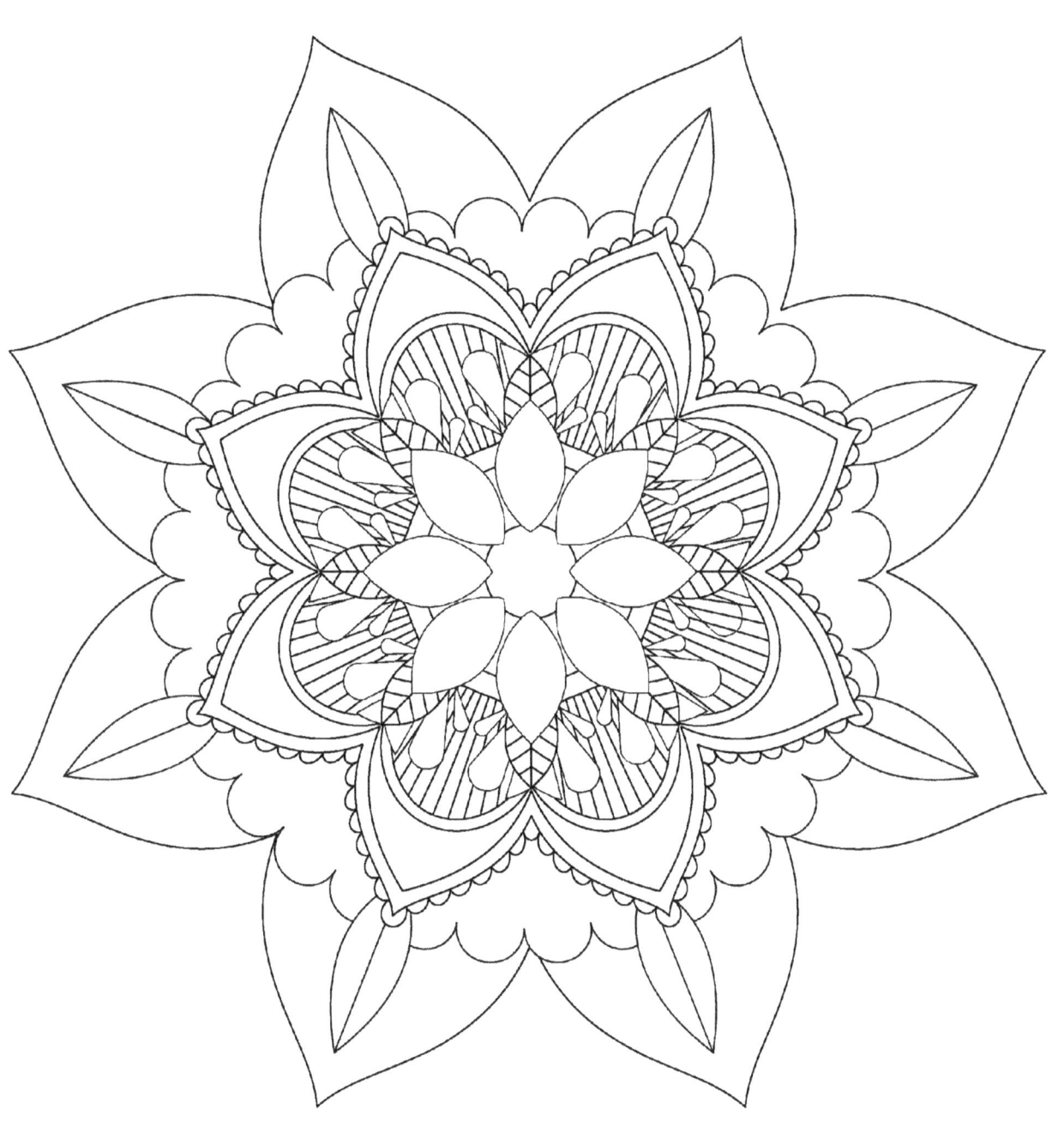

COLORS
TEST

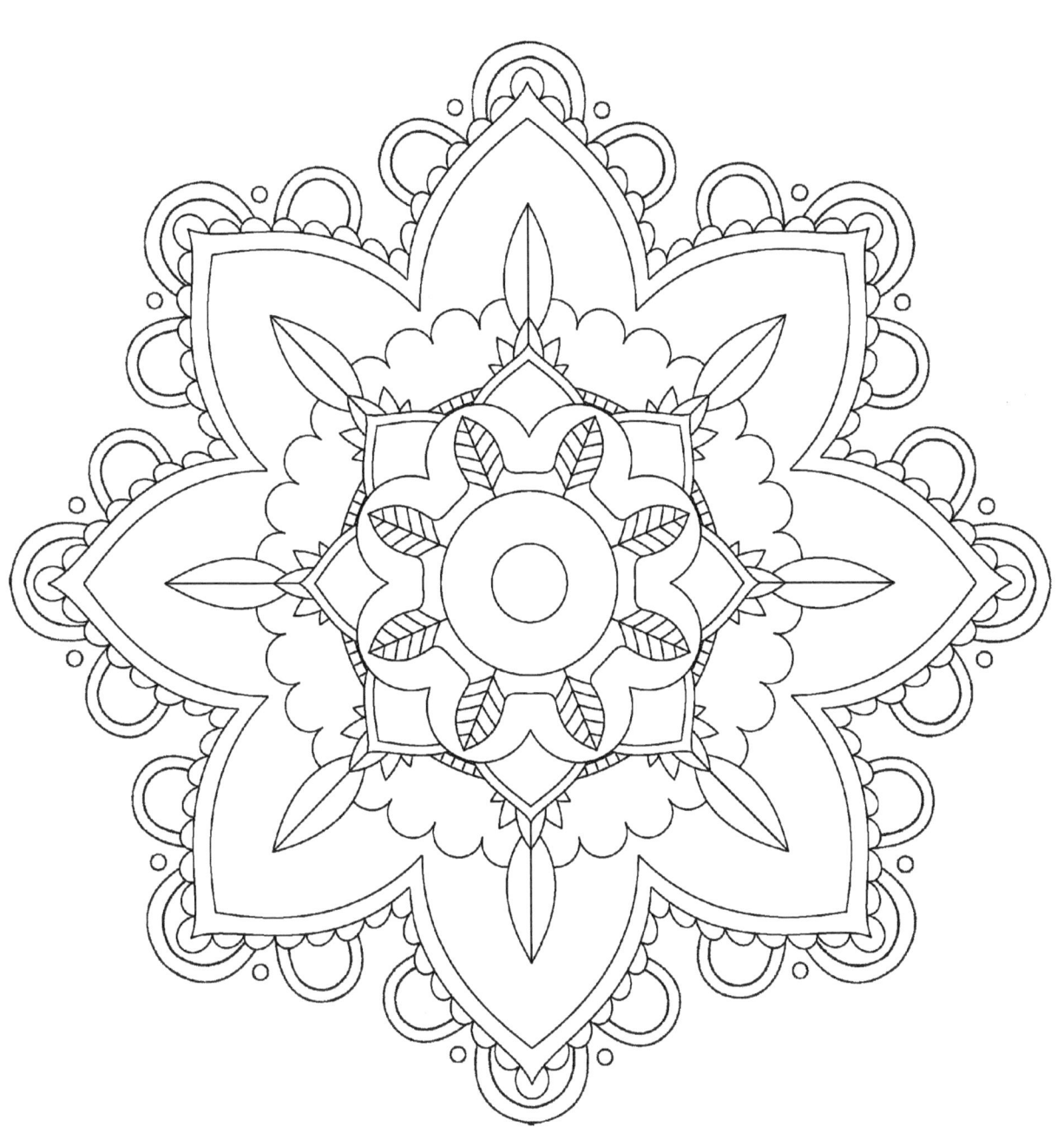

COLORS
TEST

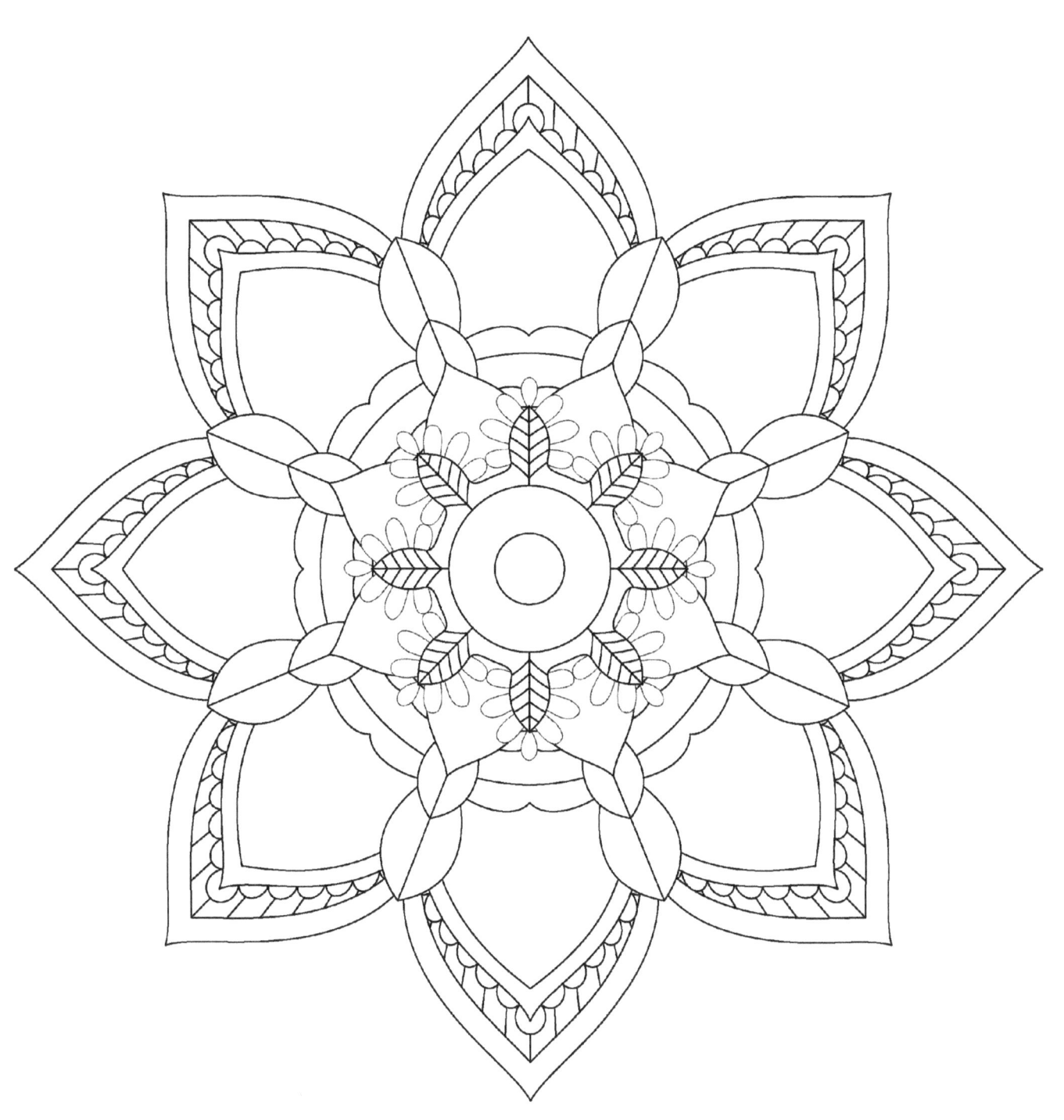

COLORS
TEST

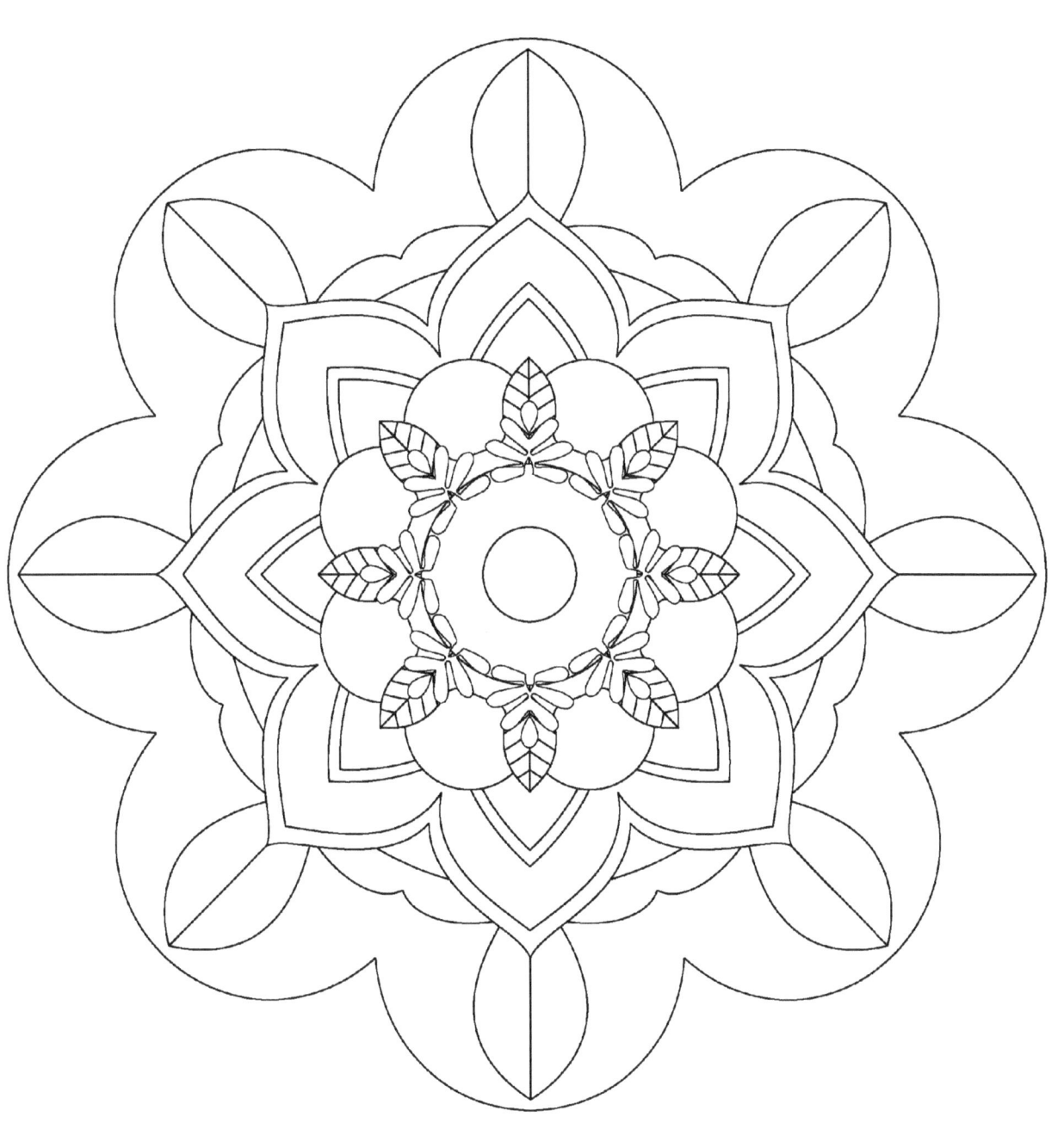

COLORS
TEST

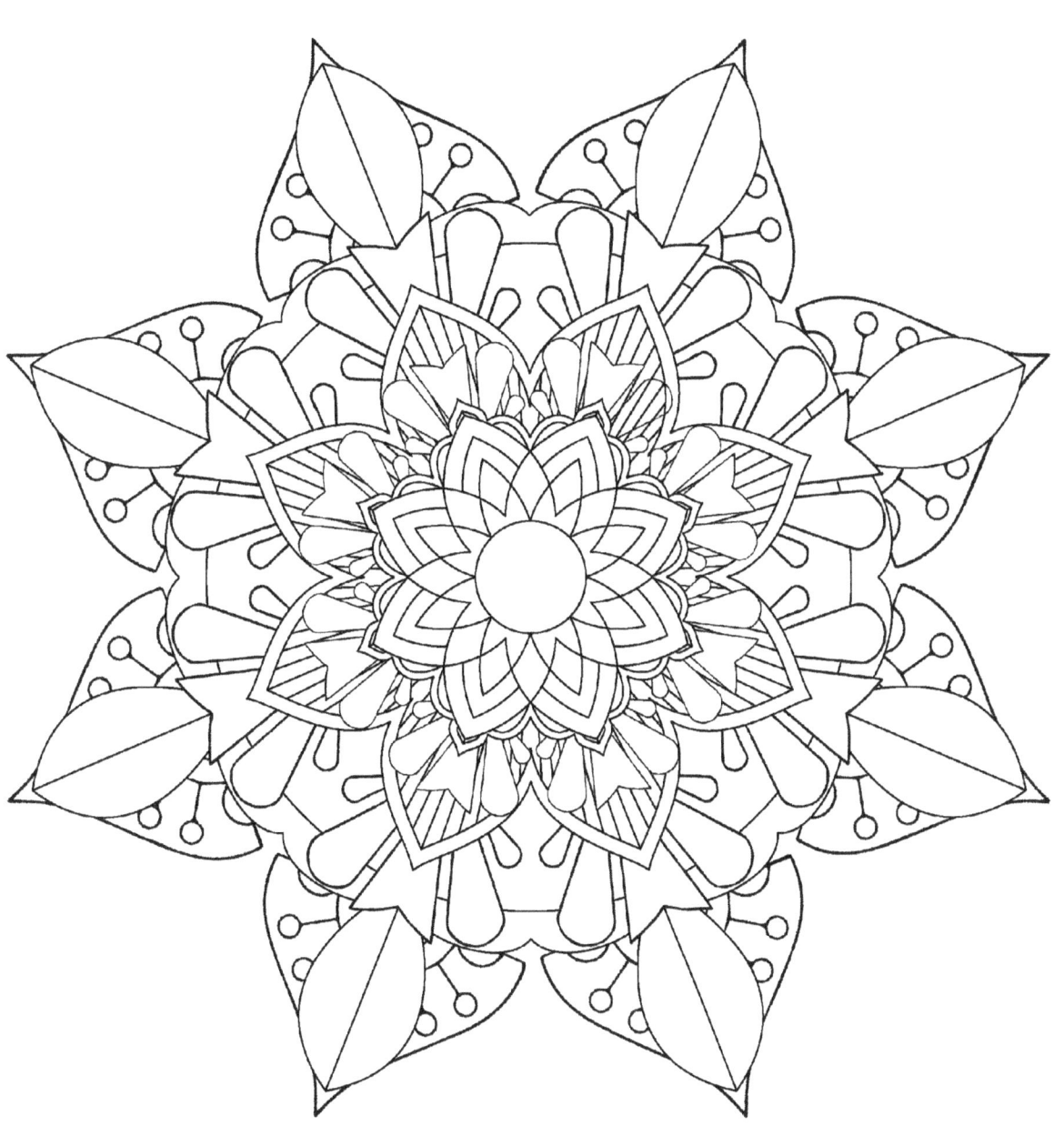

COLORS
TEST

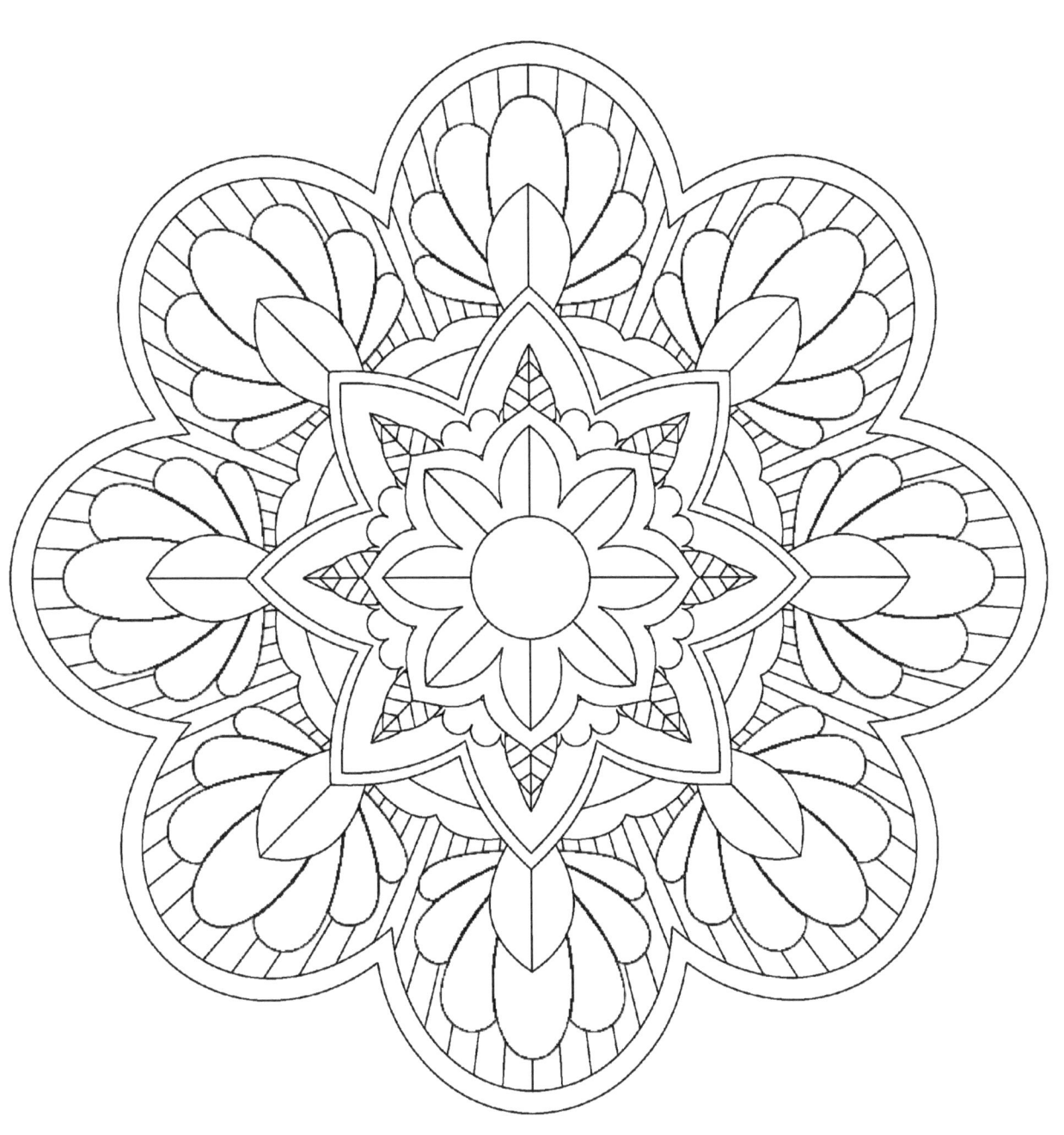

COLORS
TEST

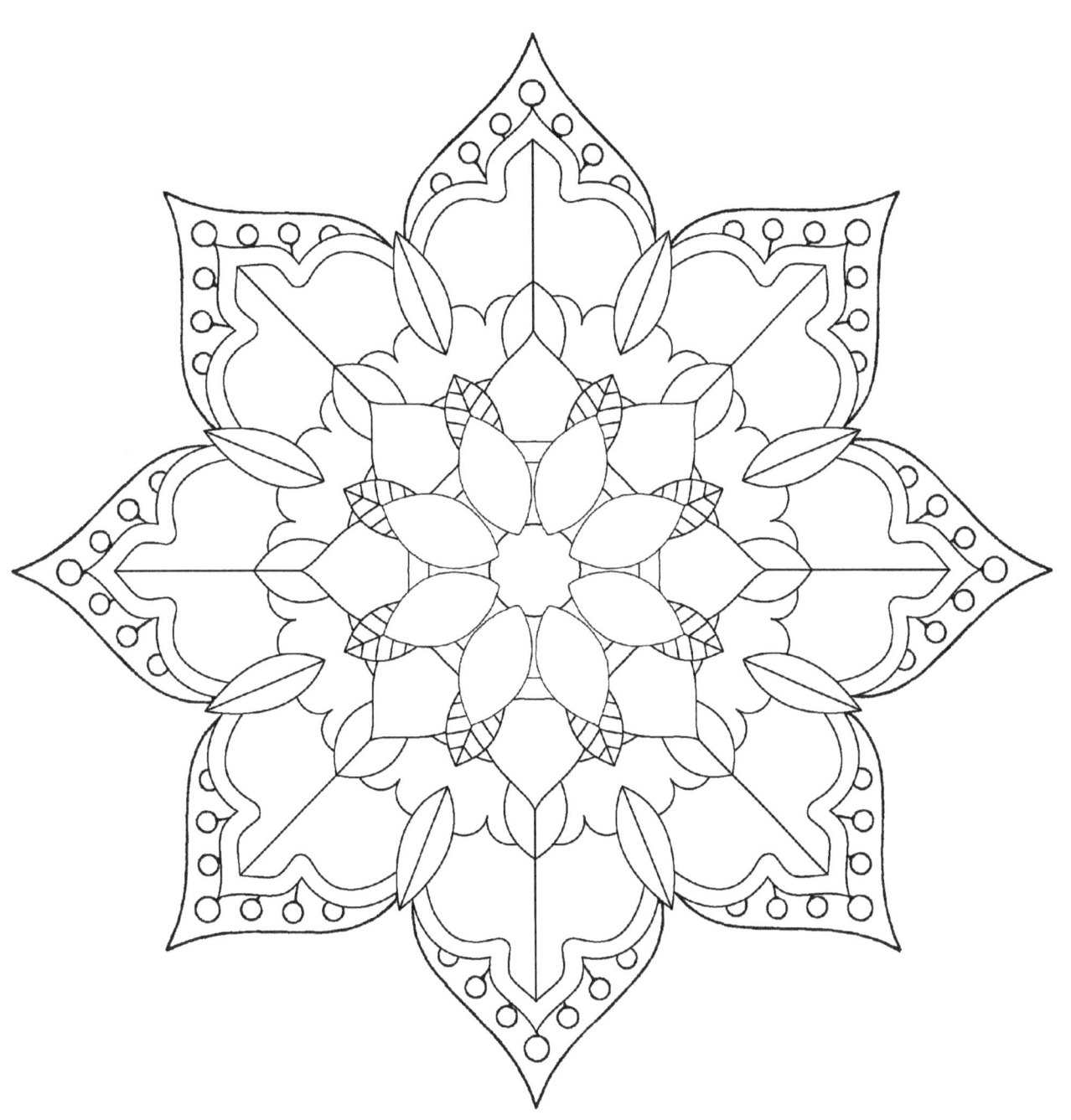

COLORS TEST

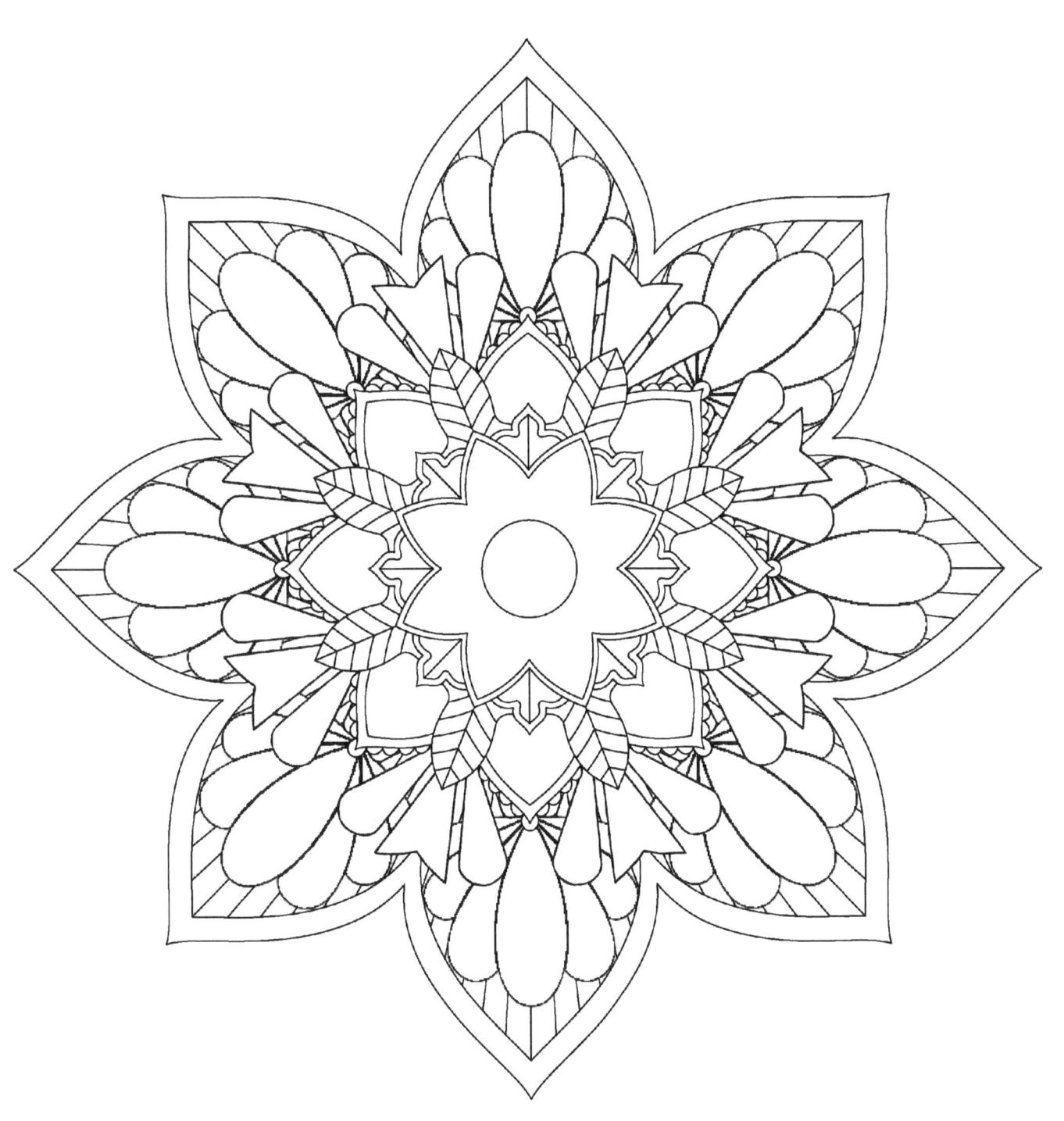

COLORS
TEST

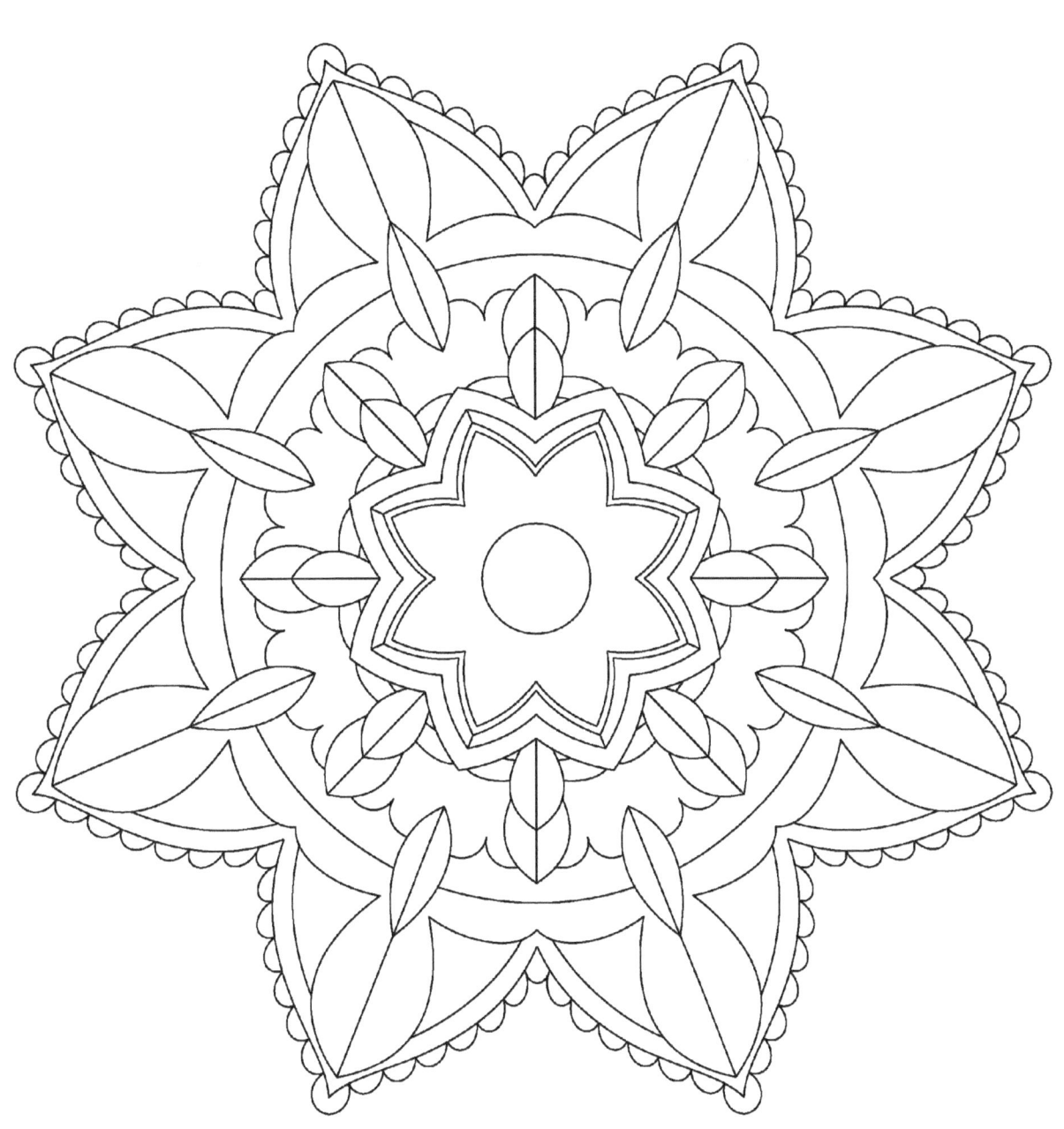

COLORS
TEST

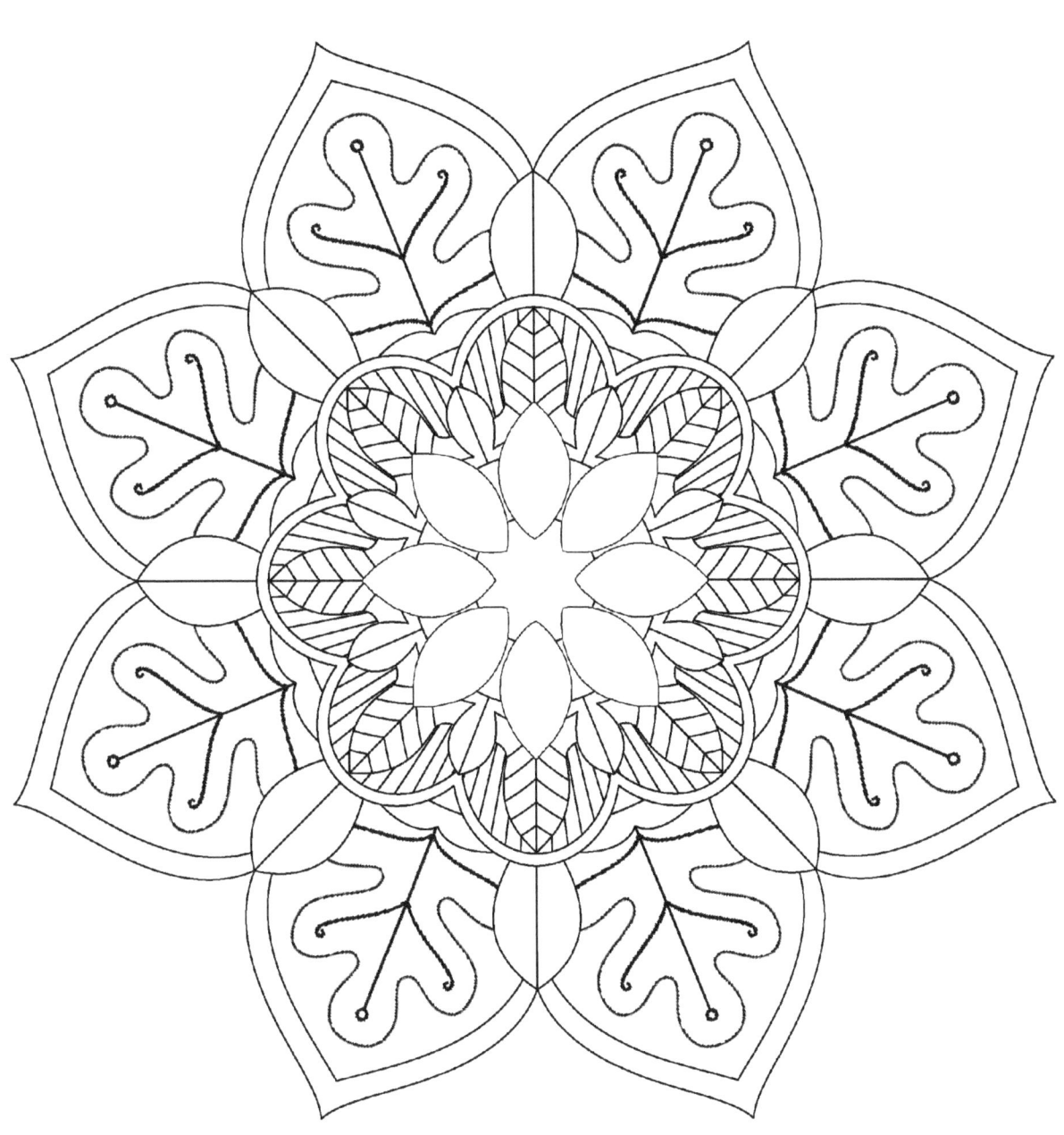

COLORS TEST

COLORS
TEST

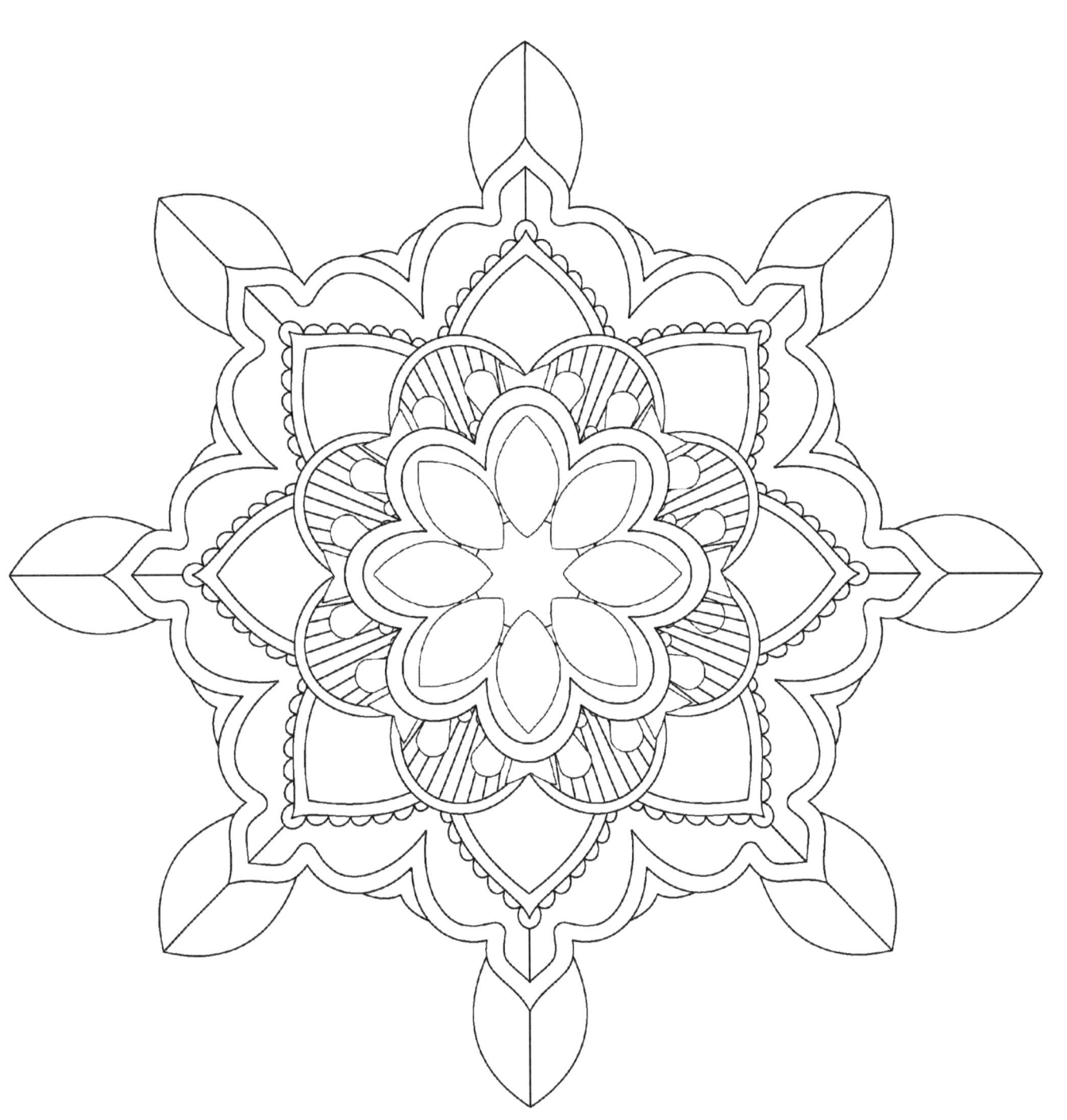

COLORS TEST

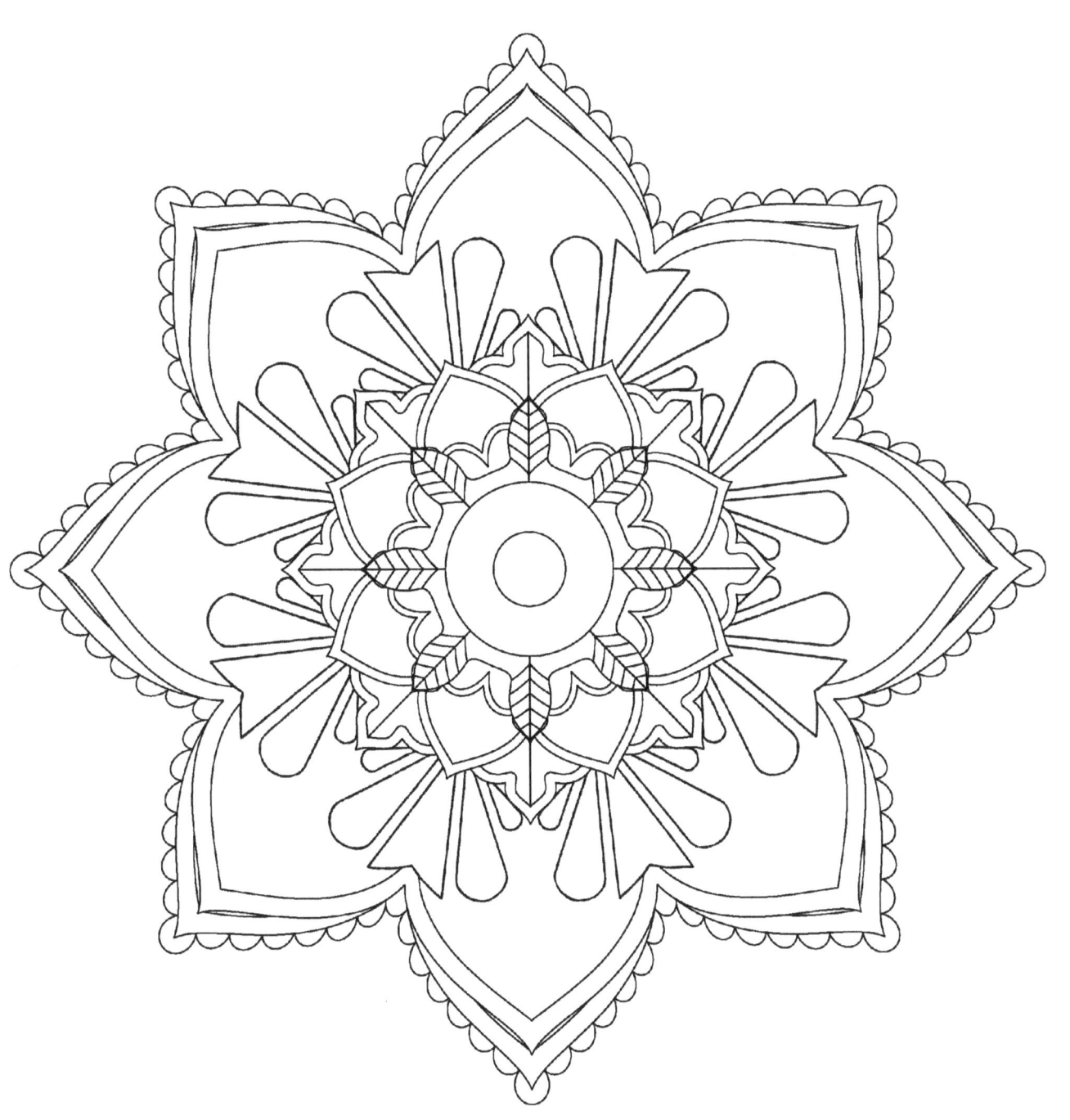

COLORS
TEST

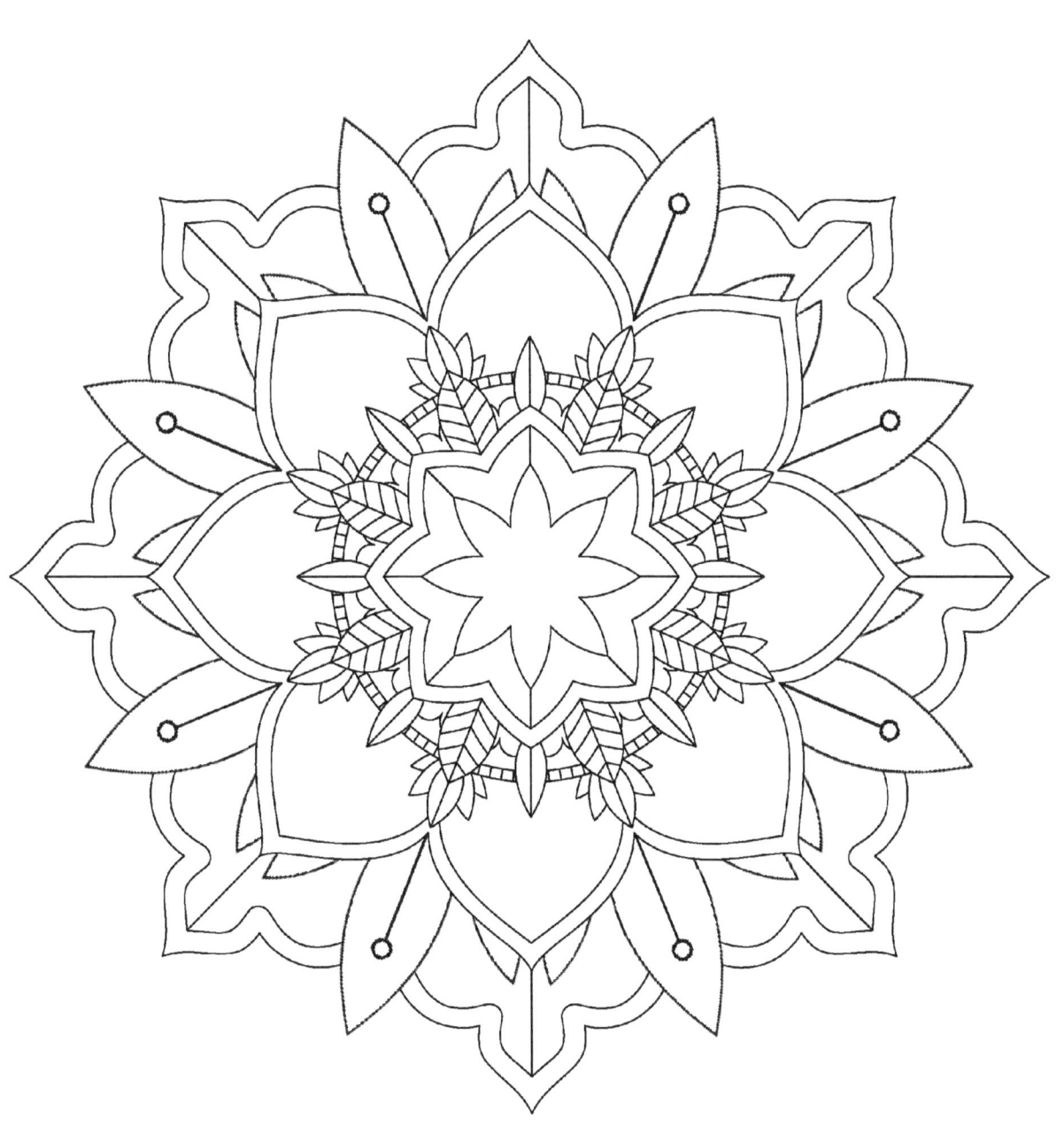

COLORS
TEST

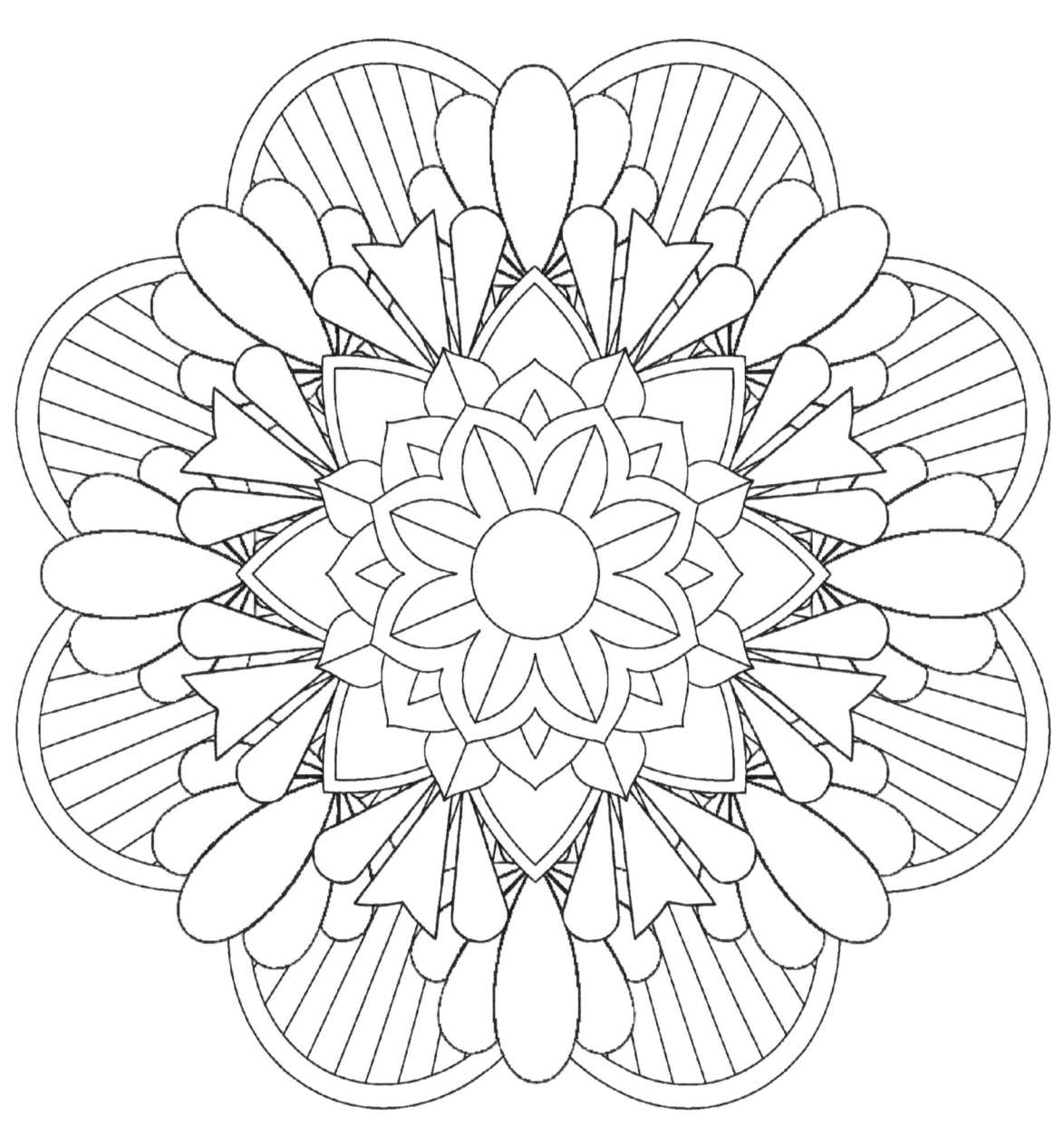

COLORS
TEST

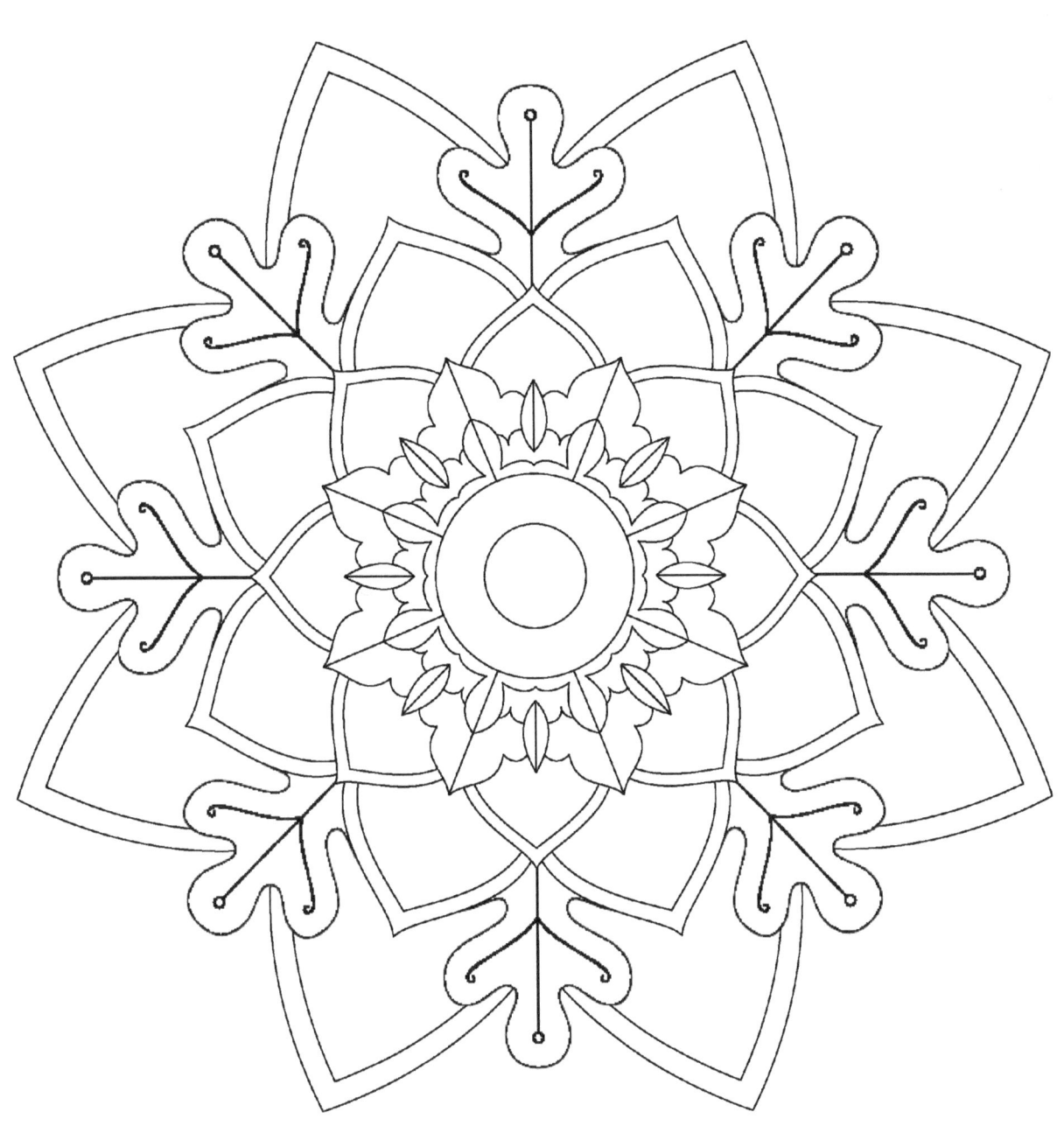

COLORS TEST

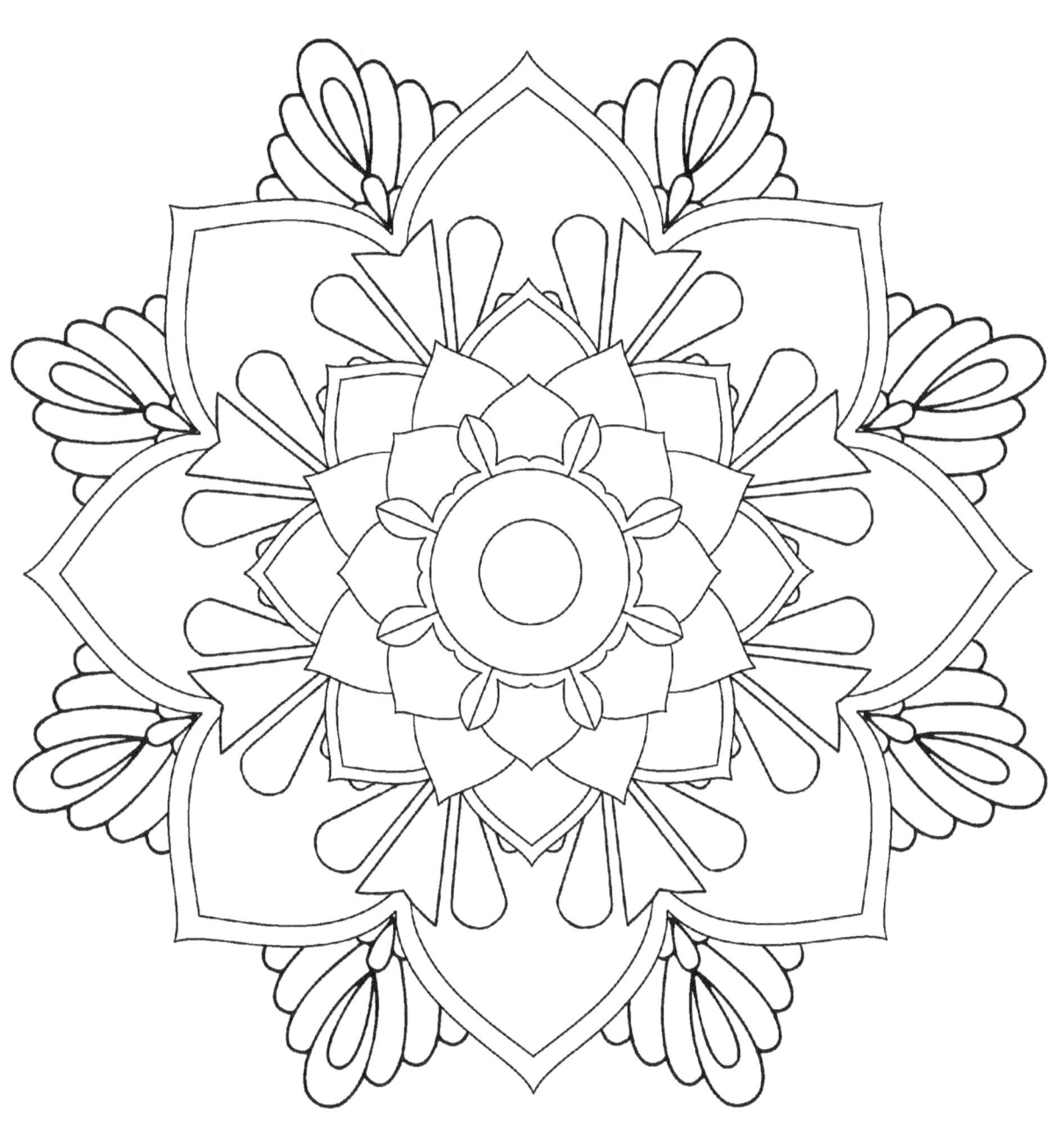

COLORS TEST

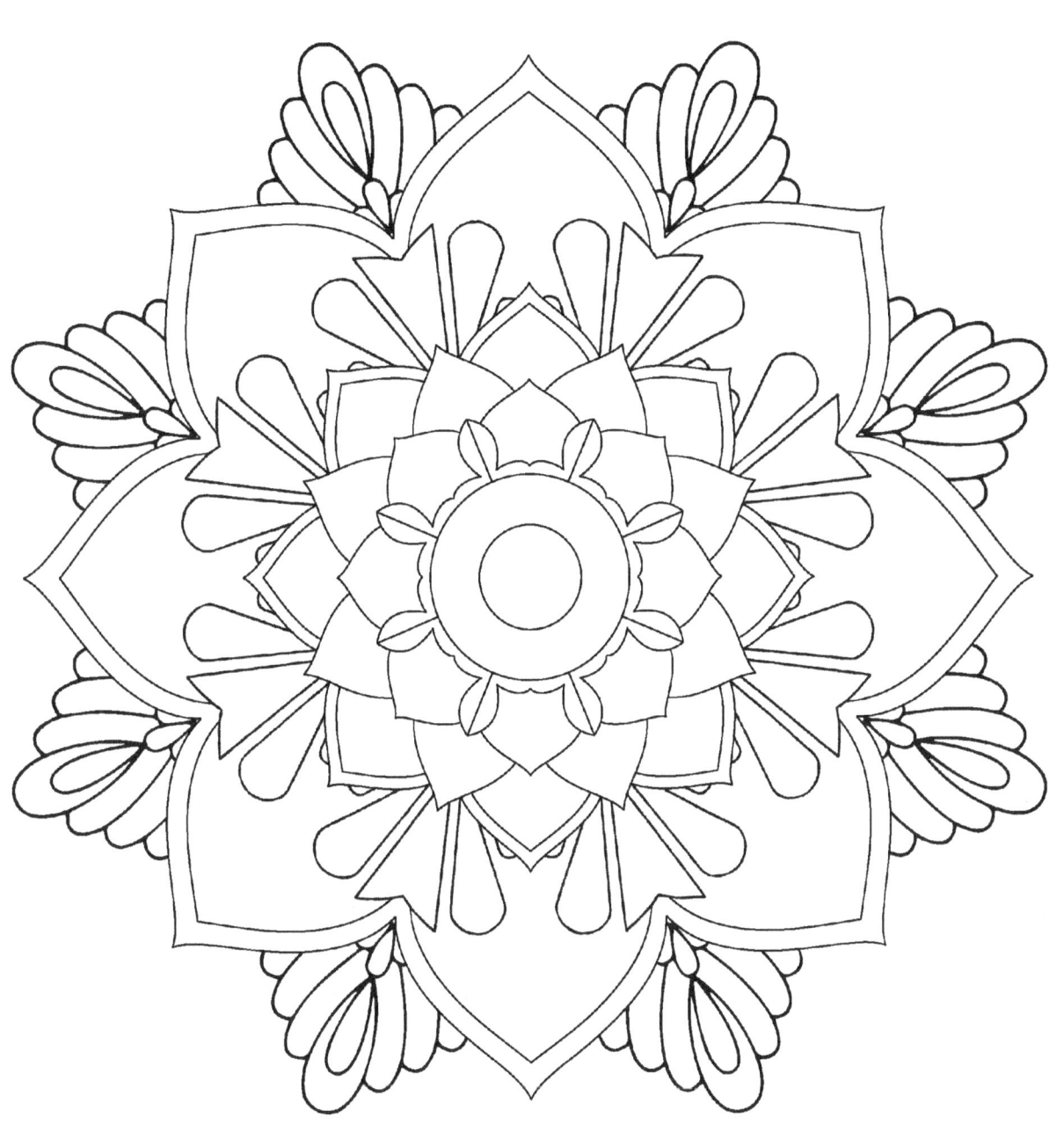

COLORS TEST

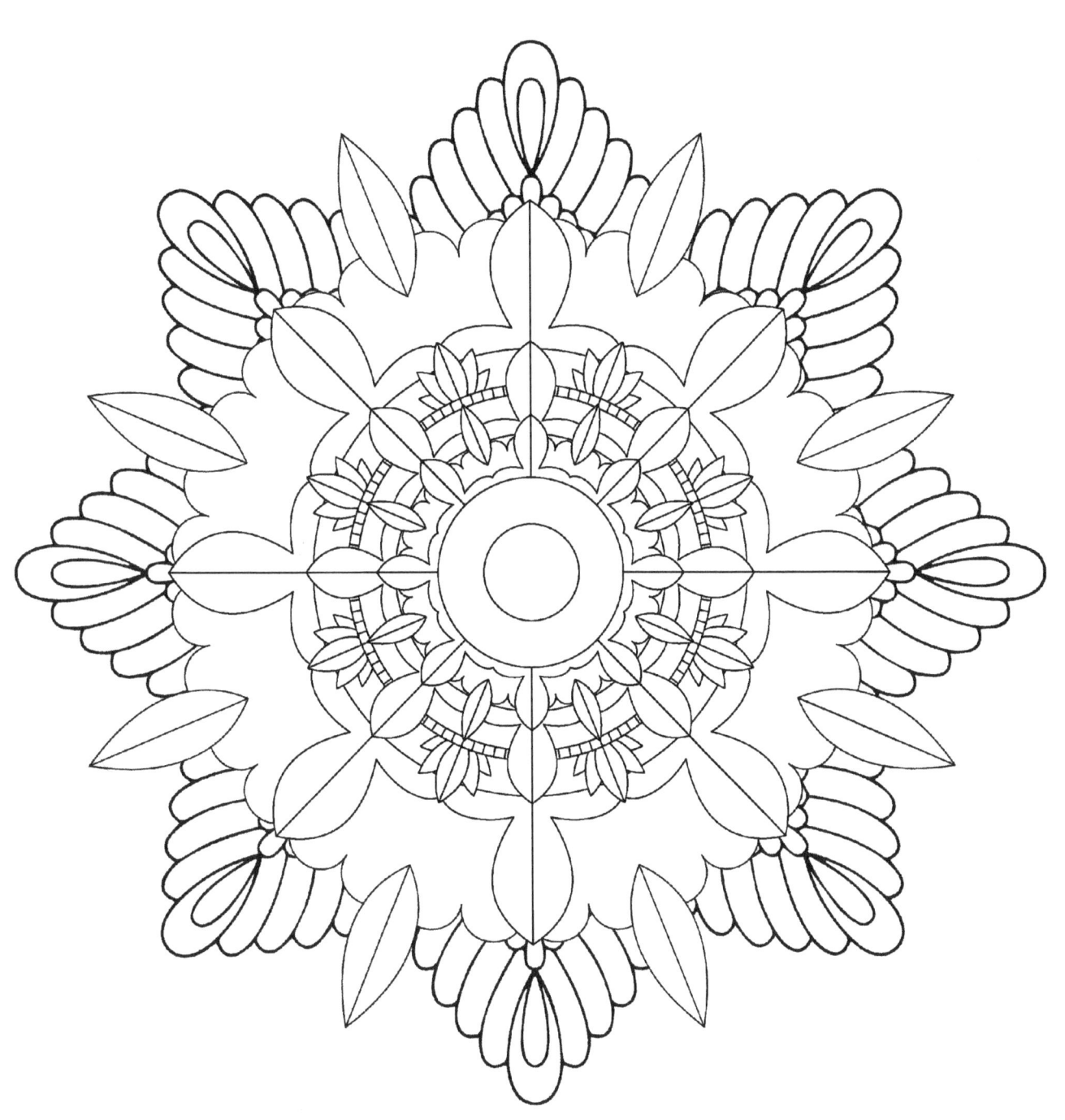

COLORS
TEST

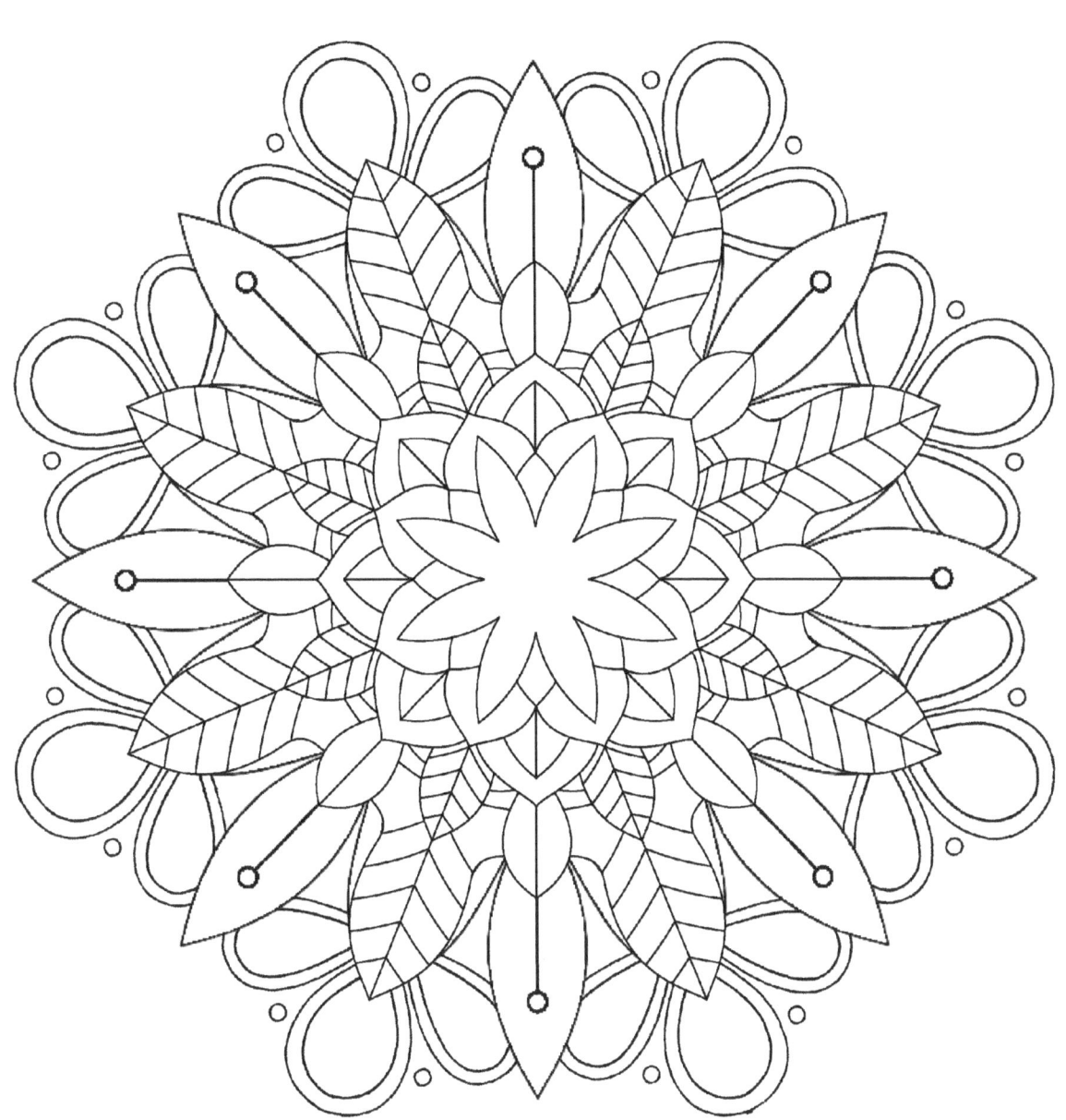

COLORS
TEST

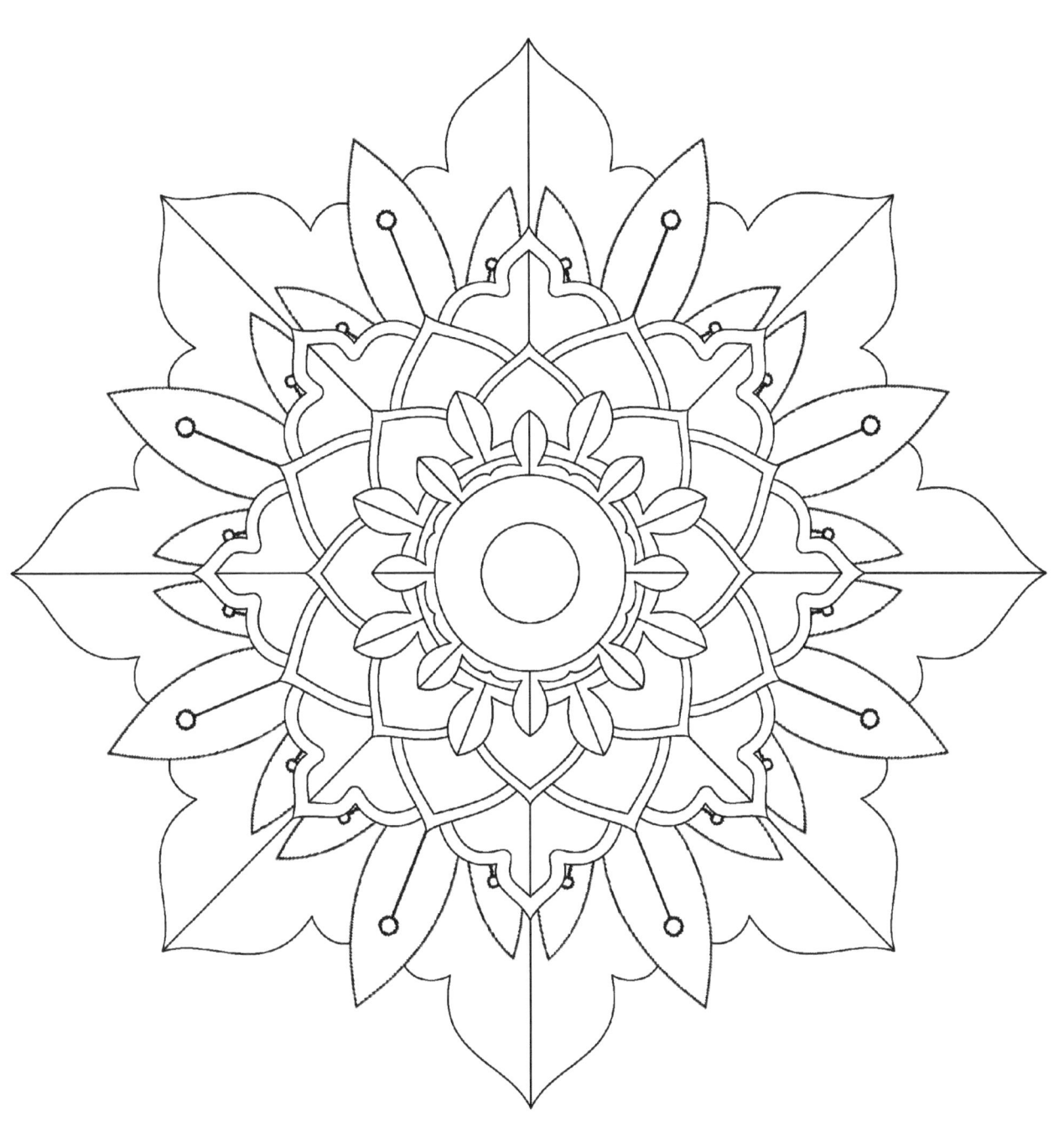

COLORS
TEST

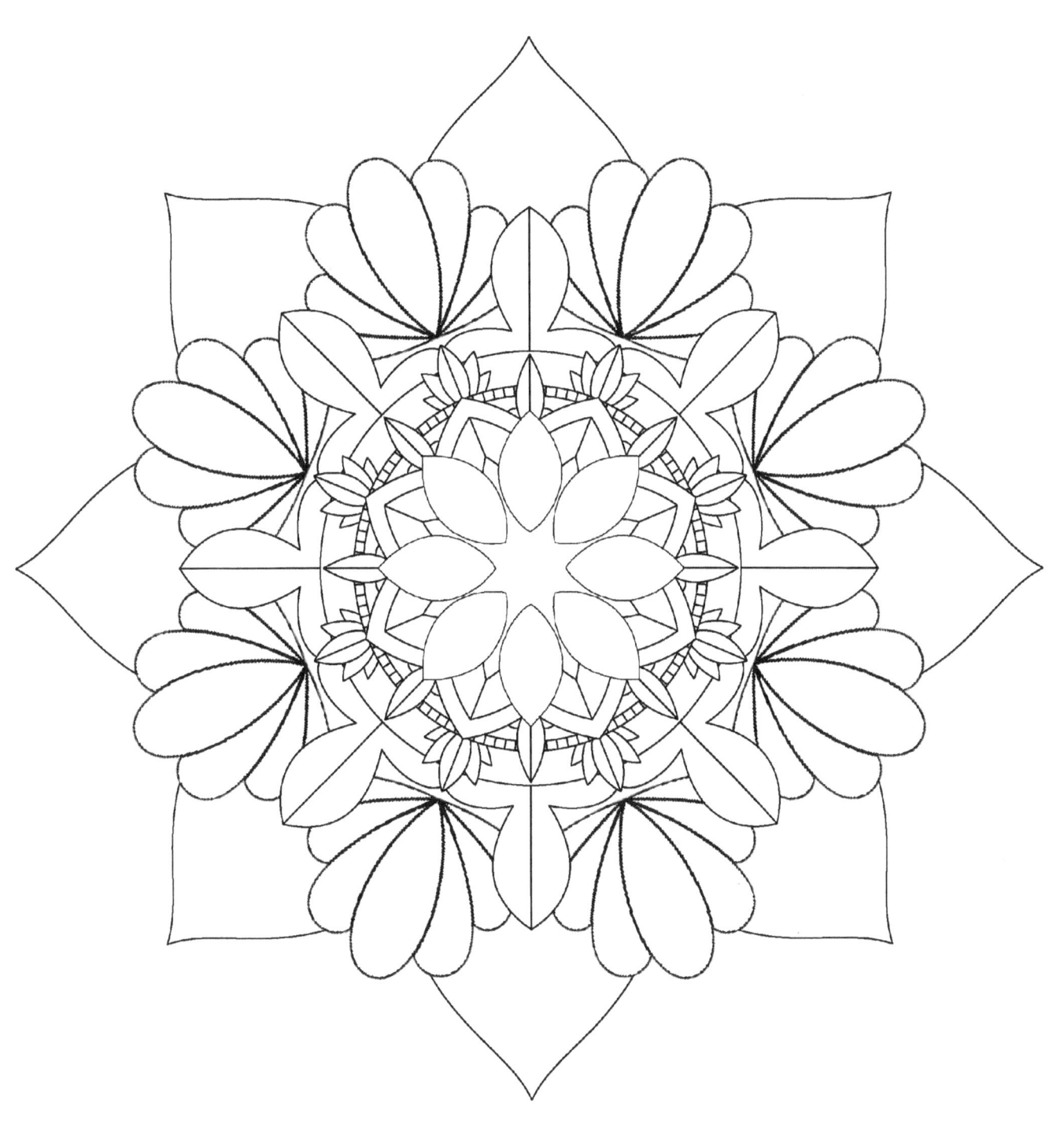

www.ingramcontent.com/pod-product-compliance
Lightning Source LLC
Chambersburg PA
CBHW080542220526
45466CB00010B/3001